Southern Living®
Cookbook
Library

The
Fondue
and Buffet
Cookbook

Cover: *Crepes Suzette (page 102)*
Left: *Chocolate-Marshmallow Fondue (page 48)*

contents

Preface 4

fondue favorites

Fondue Fundamentals 6
Meat and Seafood Fondues 11
Cheese Fondues 23
Vegetable Fondues 31
Fondue Beverages, Sauces and Desserts 39

chafing dish and oriental cookery

Chafing Dish Cookery 50
Chafing Dish Appetizers 53
Chafing Dish Vegetables, Cereals and Pastas 63
Chafing Dish Soups and Chowders 77
Chafing Dish Eggs 89
Chafing Dish Desserts 95
Chafing Dish Seafood and Poultry 105
Chafing Dish Beef, Pork and Lamb 119
Oriental Cookery 133
Oriental Cookery Know-How 134

elegant buffet specialties

Planning and Preparing Buffet Meals 142
Buffet Salads 147
Buffet Breads and Desserts 159
Buffet Casseroles 175
Index 189

preface

Southern women have long been famous for their creative cookery. But what is it that marks the difference between a good cook and a creative one?

Southern Living homemakers can tell you that creative cooks are willing to experiment with unusual and exotic ways of cooking and serving foods — and this *Fondue and Buffet Cookbook* is a tribute to their successful experiments!

Here, in one volume, hundreds of home-tested, family-approved recipes show you how to serve fondue . . . chafing dish specialties . . . buffet meals. Some of these recipes are painstakingly Americanized versions of traditional dishes from foreign cuisines. Others are developed-from-scratch originals.

You'll discover fondues ranging in flavor from smoothly mild to hotly spiced . . . chafing dish recipes to serve a few or a crowd . . . Chinese and Japanese foods offering a new universe of flavor delights . . . and buffet dishes so simple you'll wonder how you ever gave a party without them.

This is a cookbook for all occasions. It is a book you will turn to again and again when you want to transform an ordinary meal into an extra-special event. From our kitchens to yours, welcome to the wonderful world of fondue and buffet cookery — southern style!

fondue fundamentals

The word "fondue" comes from the French word "fondre," meaning to melt. The original fondue was developed in Switzerland during the 18th century. The Swiss baked bread and made cheese during the summer and fall months. This supply had to last through the long winter until the next summer. Needless to say, before the next summer the bread and cheese became very hard. Some enterprising Swiss woman hit upon the idea of melting the cheese and dipping bread chunks in it. The result: the first fondue!

EQUIPMENT

There are three types of *fondue pots*. Two are earthenware and the other is metal. Cheese fondue is traditionally prepared in a *caquelon*, a round heavy pottery dish with a wide mouth and a heavy handle such as the one shown in the illustration above.

A smaller version of this same dish is used to prepare dessert fondues.

The third type of fondue pot is a metal pot that is wider at the bottom than at the top. It is deeper than the earthenware pot. This fondue pot is used to prepare fondue Bourguignonne and vegetable fondues that require hot oil. The metal can bear the 360 degree heat needed to keep the oil hot, without cracking as would an earthenware pot. The pot's shape will help keep oil from spattering as foods are fondued. The very best metal pots are enameled steel with an extra-heavy bottom. These pots come in a wide range of brilliant colors. Other metal fondue pots may be made of stainless steel, copper, or sterling silver.

The *heat source* you choose will depend upon the kind of fondue you are preparing. Cheese, meat, seafood, and vegetable fondues need more intense heat than do dessert fondues. For the latter, choose a *candle warmer.* The dessert fondue is usually prepared on the kitchen stove over very low heat and poured into the fondue pot. The only heat source needed is one sufficient to keep the dessert warm.

For all other fondues, you may choose your heat source from alcohol lamps, canned heat, or even electricity. *Alcohol lamps* are of two types. One has a wick which is raised and lowered by a screw. The other has cotton wool in the base of the lamp. The alcohol is poured over the cotton, ignited, and the degree of heat is controlled by a cover which opens and closes vents on the side of the lamp. When using an alcohol lamp, never fill it more than half full. One tablespoon of alcohol gives about 12 minutes cooking time. Denatured alcohol is the best kind to use in these lamps: it is less expensive, produces a more intense heat, and creates less odor.

Canned heat fits into special lamps which either come with fondue pots or can be purchased separately. The degree of heat is controlled by a vented cover similar to that on the alcohol lamp. In determining how much canned heat you will need, remember that a 2 5/8-ounce can burns for 50 to 60 minutes, while a 7-ounce can burns for four hours.

Electric fondue pots are now available. To use these, simply follow the manufacturers' directions.

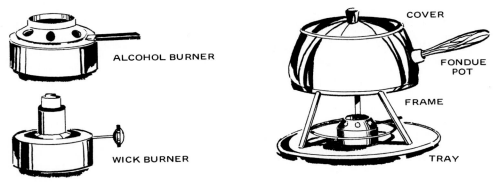

ALCOHOL BURNER

WICK BURNER

COVER

FONDUE POT

FRAME

TRAY

When you are choosing your fondue equipment, look for sturdy pots with trays to catch spills and prevent burns. Generally, one pot will comfortably serve four people — more people than that, and you will have too much confusion!

In addition to pots and heat sources, you may want to invest in special forks and plates. *Fondue forks* are usually two- or three-tined metal forks with wooden ends to prevent heat conduction. The best forks are color-keyed: each has a different color on the end so that your guests can easily tell which fork is theirs when the pot is filled with cooking food.

Fondue plates are metal, plastic, or china plates divided into several compartments. They are most often used in serving fondue Bourguignonne which is always accompanied by several sauces. The divided plates allow your guests to serve themselves with their favorite sauces and keep those sauces from blending together.

FONDUE VARIETY

In the sections that follow, recipes have been assembled for many different kinds of fondue. The classic fondue is, of course, *cheese.* The basic cheese fondue is made with two types of Swiss cheeses: Emmentaler, a mild cheese, and the stronger Gruyere. The very mildest fondue is made wholly of Emmentaler while the very strongest is made entirely of Gruyere.

Cheese for a fondue should be diced or shredded but never grated. Grating will make the cheese lump. Toss your bits of cheese with the amount of flour called for in the recipe, usually a couple of tablespoons. Be certain to use the cheese specified in your recipe. Only some cheeses can be used to prepare fondue.

To heighten flavor, rub the fondue pot lightly with half a garlic clove, then add the required amount of wine. The kind of wine you choose is important. It should be a light, dry, sparkling white wine. The Swiss prefer Neuchatel, but Rhine, Reisling, or Chablis will do as well. The wine is heated until bubbles form around the edges and on the bottom of the pot. Then add the cheese, a handful at a time, stirring constantly with a wooden spoon. When all the cheese has been added, flavor with Kirsch or brandy, if desired, and nutmeg and ground pepper.

Your guests scoop up the cheese mixture with speared pieces of crusty French or Italian bread. Each piece must have a crust so that the cheese will cling to it. The prize of the evening is the cheese crust left on the bottom of the pot: traditionally, this goes to the person who has not dropped his bread in the pot!

Fondue Bourguignonne consists of pieces of meat or seafood speared on a fork and cooked in a pot of hot cooking oil. Some cooks prefer to use a mixture of peanut oil and butter, while others use coconut oil, salad oil, or olive oil. The latter oil will smoke quickly and so it is not preferred for fondues.

The meat chosen for fondue Bourguignonne is most frequently beef — tenderloin, sirloin, or porterhouse are the preferred cuts although other cuts may be used if they are first tenderized. Veal is apt to be tough unless you use tenderloin. If you use pork, be sure to caution your guests that it must be thoroughly cooked. Allow five to seven ounces of meat per person.

Seafood may also be used. The most popular seafood fondue is shrimp: allow about two pounds of raw, shelled shrimp for four people. For other seafoods, including fish, allow the same proportions.

Each place setting should have the meat or seafood that is to be fondued served in individual bowls. For a pleasant color note, try lining each bowl with greens before filling with pieces of meat or seafood. The individual place setting should include a salad fork and a dinner fork as well as each person's fondue fork. The fondue fork is only for cooking in oil; the prongs will become too hot to eat with. You'll also want at least one dinner plate per person.

Don't forget at least four to six sauces. The best ones for meat fondue are bearnaise, chili, bottled steak sauce, horseradish, barbecue, and Cumberland. Use the same basic list for seafood fondues, substituting lemon butter and tartar sauce for the steak sauces.

Fondue International (page 13)

meat and seafood fondues

For an eye-appealing fondue treat, try the fondue known as Bourguignonne. The Swiss claim that this fondue was invented years ago in Geneva's Hotel du Rhone. Wherever it originated, this method of cooking bits of meat and seafood is universally loved today.

Into a pot of bubbling hot oil go chunks of beef, veal, or pork . . . or pieces of fish, shrimp, scallops, lobster, or crab. They are cooked amidst much laughter and camaraderie and served with a delicious wine or beverage . . . four or five favorite sauces . . . a green salad . . . and home-fried potatoes. A simple meal, yes. But it's hard to imagine anything better.

For an interesting variation, substitute boiling chicken or beef bouillon for the usual hot oil. The flavor sensations are marvelous, and the bouillon is a boon for weight-watchers and others who must be careful of their fat intake.

Southern women enjoy this casual and fun-filled way of serving family and friends and have developed many unusual and delicious recipes for fondue Bourguignonne of all types. The very best of these recipes from kitchens all over the Southland are shared with you in the pages that follow. These are the recipes that have brought delicious eating . . . and warm praise. Try one tonight — you'll see!

BEEF FONDUE WITH SAUCES

1 1/2 lb. beef tenderloin	Horseradish Cream Sauce
Salad oil	Tomato Steak Sauce
Garlic Butter	

Cut the beef in 3/4-inch cubes and let set at room temperature for about 30 minutes. Fill a metal fondue pot 1/2 full with salad oil and heat to 425 degrees. Place the fondue pot on a stand over flame. Spear beef cubes with fondue forks and cook in the oil until done. Serve with Garlic Butter, Horseradish Cream Sauce and Tomato Steak Sauce.

Garlic Butter

1/2 c. soft butter	1 clove of garlic, minced

Mix the butter and garlic in a saucepan and heat until butter is melted. Serve hot.

Horseradish Cream Sauce

1 c. sour cream	1/4 tsp. salt
3 tbsp. drained horseradish	Dash of paprika

Combine all ingredients in a bowl and mix well. Chill.

Tomato Steak Sauce

1 8-oz. can tomato sauce	2 tbsp. brown sugar
1/3 c. steak sauce	2 tbsp. salad oil

Combine all ingredients in a bowl and mix well. Chill.

Mrs. Andrew D. Hodges, Ridgeway, Virginia

BURGUNDY BEEF FONDUE

2 1/4 lb. top beef round	1/2 c. Burgundy
Salt and pepper to taste	1 c. vegetable oil
Monosodium glutamate	

Trim the beef and cut in cubes. Season with salt and pepper and sprinkle with desired amount of monosodium glutamate. Place in a shallow dish and pour the Burgundy over the beef. Let stand at room temperature for 1 hour. Pour the oil into a fondue pot and heat until very hot. Spear the beef cubes with skewers and cook in the oil until done to taste. May serve with sour cream with horseradish, chili sauce or mustard. 4 servings.

Mrs. John Melton, Bunker Hill, West Virginia

FONDUE INTERNATIONAL

4 c. corn oil	Chicken breast, boned,
Beef tenderloin or sirloin,	skinned and cut in cubes
cut in 3/4-in. cubes	Spareribs, cut in 1 1/2-in.
Leg of lamb, cut in 3/4-in.	single-rib pieces and
cubes	parboiled

Pour the corn oil into base of automatic fondue and position tray and rack. Plug unit into 120-volt outlet. Preheat oil for 10 to 15 minutes or until signal light goes on. Oil is at 375 degrees, the proper temperature for cooking. Signal light will go on and off during cooking indicating proper temperature is automatically being maintained. Follow the manufacturer's directions for cooking if your electric fondue pot differs from one pictured on page 9. Provide each person with a plate for sauces, a fondue fork for cooking meat and a separate fork for eating. Each person spears and cooks choice of meat in hot corn oil to desired doneness, lets it drain briefly on rack, then, using dinner fork, dips cooked meat into sauce. Prepare 1 1/2 to 2 pounds of 2 to 4 different meats for 4 to 5 main dish servings or 12 appetizer servings.

Chinese Plum Sauce

1 c. plum preserves or jam	1 tbsp. dry mustard
1/4 c. red wine vinegar	1/2 sm. clove of garlic,
2 tbsp. corn oil	crushed

Mix all ingredients in a bowl.

Oriental Sauce

1/2 c. mayonnaise	1 tbsp. soy sauce
1/4 c. sour cream	1 tsp. ground ginger
1/4 c. chopped green onions	

Mix all ingredients in a bowl.

Photograph for this recipe on page 9.

MARINATED STEAK FONDUE

2 lb. steak	Salad oil
4 tbsp. meat tenderizer	2 tbsp. parsley
2 tbsp. garlic salt	1/2 lb. butter
3 tbsp. cooking sherry	

Cut the steak in bite-sized cubes and place in a shallow dish. Sprinkle with meat tenderizer and garlic salt and let stand for 30 minutes. Add the sherry and 3 tablespoons salad oil and sprinkle with parsley. Marinate in the refrigerator for 3 hours. Melt the butter in a fondue pot. Add 2 cups salad oil and heat until very hot. Place the steak cubes on fondue forks and cook in the oil mixture to desired doneness. 6 servings.

Mrs. Francis Tease, Tucson, Arizona

MUSTARD-CURRY-BEEF FONDUE

Vegetable oil
2 to 3 lb. lean beef sirloin
   or tenderloin
Prepared barbecue sauce

Prepared chutney
Mustard Sauce
Curry Sauce

Fill a metal fondue pot 1/2 full with oil and heat to 400 degrees. Place on a stand over fondue burner. Cut the beef in 1-inch cubes. Spear the cubes of beef with long-handled fondue forks and cook in hot oil until done to taste. Dip cooked beef into desired sauce.

Mustard Sauce

1/4 c. prepared mustard
1/4 c. mayonnaise

1/2 clove of garlic, pressed
1/2 tsp. hot sauce

Combine all ingredients in a bowl and mix well.

Curry Sauce

1/2 c. mayonnaise
2 tbsp. milk

1 tbsp. curry powder
1/2 tsp. hot sauce

Combine all ingredients in a bowl and mix well.

Mrs. Reenie Jones, Las Vegas, Nevada

HEARTY BEEF FONDUE WITH HOT GAZPACHO SAUCE

Sirloin or tenderized round
   steak
Peanut oil
3/4 c. peeled diced tomato
1/3 c. finely diced green
   pepper
1/4 c. finely diced peeled
   cucumber
1/4 c. tomato paste
2 tbsp. finely chopped onion

1 tbsp. finely chopped
   parsley
1 tbsp. lemon juice
3/4 tsp. salt
1/4 tsp. pepper
1/2 tsp. sugar
1/4 tsp. paprika
3/4 tsp. minced garlic
1 tsp. cornstarch

Trim all the fat from steak and cut into 1-inch cubes. Dry the steak and hold at room temperature. Fill the fondue pot 2/3 full with peanut oil. Heat on burner of stove to 425 degrees or until a small piece of steak browns. Place oil on fondue stand in center of table over canned heat. Combine tomato, green pepper, cucumber, tomato paste, onion, parsley, lemon juice, 1 tablespoon peanut oil, salt, pepper, sugar, paprika and garlic in blender. Whirl just until the mixture is liquified. Stir in the cornstarch and pour into saucepan. Heat, stirring until mixture comes to a boil, then reduce the heat. Cook for 1 minute. Have each guest spear steak with long-handled fork and dip in oil, then cook to desired doneness. Dip into hot sauce.

TINY BATTERED FRANKFURTERS

1 c. milk	Salad oil
2 beaten eggs	1 tsp. salt
2 tbsp. salad oil	16 cocktail frankfurters,
1/2 tsp. prepared mustard	halved crosswise
1 1/2 c. pancake mix	

Combine first 4 ingredients in a bowl. Add the pancake mix and beat with a rotary beater until smooth. Pour enough salad oil into a fondue pot to fill to depth of 2 inches and heat to 375 degrees. Add the salt. Place the fondue pot over fondue burner. Spear a frankfurter with a fondue fork and dip into batter, letting excess run off. Fry in hot oil for about 1 minute. May be served with mustard sauce, horseradish sauce or warmed hot catsup. Frankfurters, cut in 1-inch pieces, may be substituted for cocktail frankfurters.

Mrs. Phillip Meade, Tucson, Arizona

Hearty Beef Fondue with Hot Gazpacho Sauce (page 14)

15

SIRLOIN FONDUE SUPREME

1 pkg. meat marinade mix	Cooking oil
Cooking sherry to taste	Garlic powder to taste
2 lb. tenderloin or sirloin	Nutmeg to taste

Prepare the marinade mix according to package directions, adding the sherry. Cut the tenderloin in bite-sized pieces and place in the marinade. Refrigerate for several hours or overnight. Fill a fondue pot or deep fat fryer 1/2 full with oil and heat until very hot. Place the fondue pot on a stand over a fondue burner and add the garlic powder and nutmeg to the oil. Drain the tenderloin cubes and place on fondue forks. Cook in the hot oil to desired doneness, then dip into desired sauce.

Tomato Sauce

2 tbsp. minced onion	Pinch of chopped parsley
1 tbsp. butter	1 8-oz. can tomato sauce
Pinch of sweet basil	2 tbsp. grated Parmesan cheese

Saute the onion in butter in a saucepan until tender. Add the sweet basil, parsley, tomato sauce and cheese and heat through.

Horseradish Sauce

1 c. sour cream	2 tbsp. fresh chives
1 tbsp. horseradish	

Combine all ingredients in a bowl and blend well.

Mrs. J. J. Miller, Pembroke, Virginia

MOOSE FONDUE

3 lb. moose steak	Tomato Sauce
3 c. salad oil	

Cut the steak in 1-inch cubes and let set at room temperature for about 30 minutes. Fill fondue pot 1/2 full with salad oil and heat to 375 degrees. Place steak cubes on fondue forks and cook in oil for 10 to 30 seconds. Dip into Tomato Sauce.

Tomato Sauce

1 8-oz. can tomato sauce	1/2 c. bottled steak sauce
2 tbsp. brown sugar	2 tbsp. salad oil

Combine all ingredients in a saucepan and heat through.

Mrs. Mary Melton, Wytheville, Virginia

LAMB FONDUE

1 1/2 lb. boneless leg of lamb   **Bernaise Sauce**
Salad oil

Trim the lamb and cut in 3/4-inch cubes. Let set at room temperature for 20 minutes. Pour salad oil to depth of 3 inches in a fondue pot and heat to 425 degrees. Place on a stand over fondue burner. Place cubes of lamb on fondue forks and cook in hot oil for 1 to 2 minutes or to desired doneness. Dip into Bernaise Sauce.

Bernaise Sauce

2 tbsp. dry white wine	**3 egg yolks**
1 tbsp. vinegar	**2 tbsp. water**
2 tsp. chopped onion	**1/4 tsp. salt**
1/4 tsp. tarragon leaves	**Dash of cayenne pepper**
1/2 c. butter	

Combine the wine, vinegar, onion and tarragon leaves in a saucepan and simmer until liquid is reduced to 1 tablespoon. Add the butter and heat until melted. Blend the egg yolks, water, salt and cayenne pepper in an electric blender until thick. Add hot butter mixture through hole in top of blender cover, blending on low speed. Pour into heatproof dish and keep warm over hot water, stirring occasionally.

Mrs. William G. Pouncey, Oklahoma City, Oklahoma

JET-SET FONDUE

Oil	**Shrimp, peeled and deveined**
Chicken wings, parboiled	**Beef cubes**
and tips removed	

Fill a fondue pot 1/2 full with oil and heat to 375 degrees. Place pot on stand over high flame. Place chicken wings, shrimp and beef cubes on fondue forks and cook in oil to desired doneness. Dip into sauce and serve.

Jet-Set Fondue Sauce

2 tbsp. corn oil	**1 tsp. salt**
1 clove of garlic, minced	**1 tsp. dry mustard**
1/2 c. catsup	**1 tsp. brown sugar**
1/2 c. minced onion	**1/2 tsp. hot sauce**
2 tbsp. cider vinegar	

Mix all ingredients in a small saucepan and bring to a boil over medium heat. Place in a bowl.

Photograph for this recipe on page 10.

CHICKEN FONDUE EN BARDE

3 med. cooked chicken breasts	1 tbsp. vinegar
1/4 c. soy sauce	1/4 tsp. ground ginger
2 tbsp. dry sherry	6 slices bacon
1 tbsp. sugar	Salad oil

Skin and bone the chicken breasts and cut in 3/4-inch cubes. Combine the soy sauce, sherry, sugar, vinegar and ginger in a bowl and mix well. Add the chicken and let stand for 30 minutes at room temperature, stirring occasionally. Drain well. Cut each slice bacon in thirds crosswise, then in half lengthwise. Wrap 1 piece of bacon around each chicken cube, securing with toothpicks. Chill for at least 1 hour. Pour enough salad oil into fondue pot to fill 1/2 full and heat to 375 degrees. Place the fondue pot on stand over fondue burner. Place chicken cubes on long skewers and cook in hot oil for about 1 minute or until the bacon is cooked. 36 appetizers.

Mrs. Lois Osborne, Lanett, Alabama

DELICIOUS CORNED BEEF BALLS

1 3-oz. package cream cheese	1/2 c. all-purpose flour
1 tsp. instant minced onion	1/2 c. evaporated milk
1 16-oz. can sauerkraut	Salad oil
1 12-oz. can corned beef	1 tsp. salt
1 c. fine dry bread crumbs	

Soften the cream cheese in a bowl. Add the onion and mix well. Drain the sauerkraut well, then chop. Add to the cream cheese mixture. Add the corned beef and 1/4 cup bread crumbs and mix well. Shape into 1-inch balls and roll in the flour. Dip into the milk, then roll in remaining bread crumbs. Pour salad oil into a fondue pot to depth of 2 inches and heat to 375 degrees. Add the salt. Place the fondue pot over fondue burner. Spear each corned beef ball with a fondue fork and fry in hot oil for 1 to 2 minutes.

Mrs. Patty Bryant, Roswell, New Mexico

ROMANO SHRIMP FONDUE

3/4 lb. fresh shrimp	1/2 c. grated Romano cheese
2 tbsp. butter or margarine	1/8 tsp. paprika
2 tbsp. flour	Dash of cayenne pepper
1/4 tsp. salt	Carrot, cucumber and
1 1/4 c. half and half	celery sticks
1 tbsp. dry sherry	

Cook the shrimp in enough boiling, salted water to cover just until shrimp turn pink. Shell and devein. Melt the butter in a fondue pot over low heat. Stir in the flour and salt and cook until bubbly. Add the half and half gradually and cook, stirring, until thickened and smooth. Blend in the sherry, cheese, paprika and cayenne pepper. Stir in the shrimp and place over low burner. Dip vegetable sticks into fondue.

Mrs. Tom Johnston, Atlanta, Georgia

SALMON FONDUE

2 tbsp. butter or margarine	1 c. milk
3 tbsp. flour	1 1/2 c. grated Swiss cheese
1 7 3/4-oz. can salmon	Dash of hot sauce
Bottled clam juice	French bread, cut in chunks

Melt the butter in a fondue pot over a burner and stir in the flour. Drain the salmon and reserve liquid. Add enough clam juice to reserved liquid to make 1/2 cup liquid. Stir into the flour mixture. Add the milk and cook until smooth and thickened, stirring constantly. Add the cheese and stir until cheese is melted. Flake the salmon and add to sauce. Stir in the hot sauce and cook for 5 minutes. Turn flame to low. Serve fondue with French bread and lobster chunks.

Salmon Fondue (above)

FISH AND SHRIMP FONDUE

1 1-lb. slice salmon, 1/2 to 3/4 in. thick Cooking oil	1 lb. shelled deveined shrimp

Cut the salmon into 2 x 1/4-inch strips. Fill metal fondue pot 1/2 full with oil and heat to 350 degrees. Place the fondue pot on stand over moderately high flame. Loop fish strip onto long, heavy bamboo skewer and cook in hot oil until done and lightly browned. Place shrimp on bamboo skewers and cook in hot oil until pink. Cool slightly and serve with curry sauce, tartar sauce or desired seafood sauce. Halibut may be substituted for salmon.

Mrs. George Dalziel, Norfolk, Virginia

LOBSTER FONDUE

1 10-oz. can frozen cream of shrimp soup, thawed 1/4 c. milk or half and half 1 7 1/2-oz. can lobster	1/2 c. shredded American process cheese 2 tsp. lemon juice Dash of paprika Dash of white pepper

Combine the soup and milk in a fondue pot and heat through, stirring frequently. Drain and flake the lobster and add to soup mixture. Fold in remaining ingredients and heat to serving temperature over low flame. Serve as appetizer with melba toast. May be served as luncheon dish on toast points or in patty shells, adding more milk if needed.

Mrs. Stanley Krug, Scottsdale, Arizona

TOASTED CREVETTES

1 lb. peeled cleaned fresh shrimp 3 tbsp. finely chopped onion 1 egg, beaten 1 tbsp. flour	2 tsp. lemon juice 3/4 tsp. salt Dash of pepper 6 slices bread Salad oil

Grind or blend the shrimp. Add the onion, egg, flour, lemon juice, salt and pepper and mix well. Trim crusts from the bread and cut each slice into 4 pieces. Spread shrimp mixture on both sides of bread. Pour enough salad oil into fondue pot to fill 1/2 full and heat to 375 degrees. Place over fondue burner. Spear the shrimp bread with a fondue fork and fry in hot oil for 1 to 2 minutes. 24 appetizers.

Mrs. Bob Summers, Dallas, Texas

FISH-SHRIMP FONDUE

Butter Oil Chunks of halibut or mackerel	Fresh shrimp, shelled and deveined Sweet and Tangy Sauce Piquant Sauce

Combine equal parts butter and oil to a depth of 2 inches in electric skillet or metal fondue pot and heat to 360 degrees. Spear the fish and shrimp on fondue forks and cook in butter mixture until done to taste. Serve with Sweet and Tangy Sauce, Piquant Sauce and sliced crusty bread or rolls. Your favorite meats may also be used for fonduing.

Sweet And Tangy Sauce

1 tbsp. cornstarch	1/4 c. prepared mustard
1/2 c. orange juice	1/4 tsp. ground ginger
1/2 c. honey	

Place the cornstarch in a small saucepan and add orange juice gradually, stirring to blend completely. Add the honey, mustard and ginger and heat to boiling point. Cook, stirring constantly, until thickened. Serve warm or at room temperature.

Piquant Sauce

1 c. chili sauce	1 tbsp. Worcestershire sauce
1 to 2 tbsp. prepared horseradish	

Combine the chili sauce, horseradish and Worcestershire sauce in a bowl and mix well.

Fish-Shrimp Fondue (page 20)

21

cheese fondues

Mouth-watering cheese fondue! Since its beginning hundreds of years ago as the thrifty dish of Swiss peasants, cheese fondue has been transformed into a real gourmet treat, featured at thousands of dining tables all over the world.

Now, you and your guests can share this world of great cheese fondues. In the pages that follow, the readers of *Southern Living* pass on to you their most compliment-winning cheese fondue recipes.

These women suggest that to get the most from their recipes, you remember a few easy cooking and serving hints. Always cook cheese fondue over a low flame as it toughens if the temperature is too high. Despite your care, the cheese mixture may separate. If this happens, add about one-quarter cup warm wine.

With any of these delicious recipes, serve parsley-boiled potatoes . . . saffron rice . . . or a crisp green salad with your very best creamy dressing. Do serve a warm beverage: cold drinks and cheese fondue are a poor combination. And include candles among your table decorations — they add so much to the convivial atmosphere which is an important part of fondue fun!

The next time you want to make an extra-special impression on family and guests, try serving a cheese fondue. You'll be getting compliments for weeks afterward!

PAT'S FONDUE SAVANT

1/2 stick butter	8 slices American cheese, cubed
3 tbsp. flour	Minced garlic to taste
1 1/2 c. milk	Minced onion to taste
1 can Cheddar cheese soup	Seasoned salt to taste

Melt the butter in a fondue pot and stir in the flour. Add the milk slowly and cook, stirring, until thickened. Add soup, cheese, garlic, onion and salt and cook over low heat, stirring frequently, until cheese is melted. Place pot on stand over low flame. Place cauliflowerets, rolled pepperoni slices and mushroom buttons on fondue forks and dip into fondue.

Photograph for this recipe on page 5.

QUICK CHEESE FONDUE

1 can Cheddar cheese soup	French bread, cut in cubes

Heat the soup in a fondue pot and place over low flame. Place bread cubes on fondue forks and dip into soup.

Mrs. Juliet Adams, Louisville, Kentucky

CHEESE FONDUE AU VIN

1 c. wine	1/8 tsp. garlic powder
1 lb. Swiss cheese, grated	1 c. margarine
1/2 tsp. Worcestershire sauce	1 c. shortening
1/8 tsp. nutmeg	Bread cubes

Heat the wine in a fondue pot. Add the cheese, Worcestershire sauce, nutmeg and garlic powder and heat, stirring, until cheese is melted. Place over low flame and keep hot. Heat the margarine and shortening in another fondue pot and fry bread in margarine mixture until browned. Dip bread into cheese mixture.

Barbara Sawyer, Memphis, Tennessee

CLASSIC SPICED CHEESE FONDUE

3/4 lb. Swiss cheese	Dash of pepper
1 tbsp. all-purpose flour	Dash of nutmeg
1 clove of garlic, split	3 tbsp. dry sherry
1/4 clove of garlic, minced	1 loaf French bread, cut in
1 1/4 c. sauterne	cubes

Cut the cheese in thin strips and place in a sack. Add the flour and toss to coat. Rub inside of a fondue pot with split clove of garlic and sprinkle in minced garlic. Pour the sauterne into the pot and heat until bubbles start to rise. Do not cover or boil. Add cheese gradually, and cook, stirring constantly until melted. Stir in the pepper, nutmeg and sherry and place over flame. Add warmed sauterne if mixture becomes thick. Dip bread cubes into fondue.

Mrs. Alan McCarthy, Mobile, Alabama

CRAB RAREBIT FOR BUFFET

6 tbsp. butter	1 lb. sharp Cheddar cheese,
2 tbsp. flour	grated
1/2 tsp. dry mustard	1 tsp. Worcestershire sauce
1/4 c. cream	2 cans crab meat
1/4 c. sherry	Melba toast

Melt the butter in a fondue pot. Stir in the flour and mustard until smooth. Add the cream, sherry, cheese and Worcestershire sauce and cook over low heat, stirring, until cheese is melted. Add the crab meat and additional cream or sherry, if needed, and heat through. Place fondue pot on a stand over flame. Serve crab mixture with melba toast.

Mrs. Furman H. Green, Wilmington, Delaware

TUNA-CHEESE FONDUE

1 clove of garlic, halved	2 tbsp. kirsch or brandy
2 c. dry white wine	Dash of nutmeg
1/2 lb. Swiss cheese, diced	1 6 1/2 or 7-oz. can tuna
1/2 lb. Gruyere cheese, diced	Cubes of French or Italian
1 1/2 tbsp. cornstarch	bread

Rub inside of fondue pot with garlic. Add the wine and warm over medium heat. Do not boil. Add cheeses gradually and stir until cheese melts and mixture begins to boil. Blend the cornstarch, kirsch and nutmeg and stir into cheese mixture. Drain and flake the tuna and add to cheese mixture. Cook, stirring constantly, for 1 minute. Place over heating unit of pot and serve with bread cubes. 4 servings.

MUSHROOM-CHEDDAR FONDUE

1 can Cheddar cheese soup	Bread, cut in bite-sized
1 can golden mushroom soup	pieces
1 sm. roll garlic cheese	

Place the soups and cheese in a fondue pot and cook over low flame, stirring, until cheese is melted. Dip the bread in cheese mixture and serve.

Jacquelyn Vogt, Cape Kennedy, Florida

Geneva Fondue (below)

GENEVA FONDUE

1 clove of garlic, split	**1 tbsp. cornstarch**
2 c. dry white wine or apple juice	**3 tbsp. kirsch or lemon juice**
1/2 lb. Emmentaler cheese, finely shredded	**Nutmeg, pepper or paprika to taste**
1/2 lb. natural Gruyere cheese. finely shredded	**French bread, cut in chunks**

Rub inside of fondue pot with garlic. Pour the wine into the pot and place over low heat until bubbles rise to surface. Add the cheeses, 1 spoon at a time, stirring constantly with wooden spoon, and cook until cheese is melted. Blend the cornstarch and kirsch and stir into cheese mixture. Add the nutmeg and stir until smooth and thickened. Place fondue pot over flame. Serve fondue with French bread. May be prepared with 1 pound Emmentaler cheese instead of both Emmentaler and Gruyere cheese. In Switzerland, according to tradition, you must stir Cheese Fondue as you dip the bread, drawing the figure 8, thus representing the Swiss Flag which is shown in this photograph. 3 servings.

FAMILY-STYLE SWISS CHEESE FONDUE

3 tbsp. butter or margarine	**1/2 tsp. garlic salt**
3 tbsp. flour	**1/2 tsp. salt**

Dash of white pepper
Dash of nutmeg
2 1/2 c. milk
1 lb. Swiss process cheese,
  shredded

1 tsp. Worcestershire sauce
Dash of hot sauce
French bread, cut in
  1-in. cubes

Melt the butter in a fondue pot over moderate heat. Stir in the flour, garlic salt, salt, pepper and nutmeg. Stir in the milk and cook, stirring constantly, until smooth and slightly thickened. Add the cheese, a small amount at a time, and cook over low heat, stirring, until cheese is melted. Stir in remaining ingredients except bread. Spear cube of bread with fondue fork and twirl bread in cheese mixture until coated. Cool slightly.

Mrs. B. E. Bridges, Annandale, Virginia

FONDUE NEUCHATEL-STYLE

1 lb. Gruyere cheese, grated
3 tbsp. flour
1 clove of garlic, split
2 c. dry white wine
1 tbsp. lemon juice

3 tbsp. kirsch
1/4 tsp. nutmeg
1 tsp. pepper
2 loaves day-old bread

Mix the cheese with flour. Rub a fondue pot with garlic. Pour in the white wine and place over moderate heat until air bubbles rise to the surface. Add the lemon juice. Add the cheese, small amount at a time, and cook, stirring constantly, until the cheese is melted. Add the kirsch, nutmeg and pepper and stir until blended. Place fondue pot over flame. Cut the bread in 1-inch cubes. Place cubes on fondue forks and dip into fondue mixture.

Mrs. Susan Peterson, Anderson, South Carolina

ITALIAN FONDUE

1/4 lb. ground beef
1/2 env. spaghetti sauce mix
1 15-oz. can tomato sauce
3 c. shredded Cheddar cheese
1 c. shredded mozzarella cheese

1 tbsp. cornstarch
1/2 c. Chianti
Italian bread, cut in
  bite-sized pieces

Brown the ground beef in a saucepan and drain off excess fat. Stir in the spaghetti sauce mix and tomato sauce. Add the cheeses gradually and cook over low heat, stirring, until cheeses are melted. Blend the cornstarch with Chianti and stir into cheese mixture. Cook and stir until thickened and bubbly. Pour into a fondue pot and place over fondue burner. Spear bread cube with fondue fork and dip into beef mixture, swirling to coat. Add a small amount of Chianti if fondue becomes thick. About 6 servings.

Mrs. Olean McGuire, Jacksonville, Florida

HOT CHEESE DIP

2 tbsp. minced onion	2 c. shredded American
1 tbsp. butter	process cheese
1 tsp. mayonnaise	2 2 1/4-oz. cans deviled ham
1/2 c. tomato juice	Dash of hot sauce

Saute the onion in butter in a fondue pot over low heat until onion is transparent. Add remaining ingredients and stir until cheese is melted and ingredients are combined. Place over candle warmer. Swirl bread sticks in cheese mixture until lightly coated. Add more tomato juice if dip becomes too thick. 2 cups.

Photograph for this recipe on page 22.

NIPPY CHEESE FONDUE

2 loaves French bread	2 tbsp. Worcestershire sauce
2 cans frozen cream of	2 sm. cans deveined shrimp,
shrimp soup	drained
2 rolls nippy cheese	

Cut the bread in wedges and toast. Place the soup and cheese in a fondue pot and cook over low flame, stirring, until cheese is melted. Add the Worcestershire sauce and shrimp and heat through. Place over flame. Serve with bread.

Mrs. Frank Mitchell, Richmond, Virginia

PIZZA-CHEESE FONDUE

1 env. onion soup mix	1 1/2 c. grated Cheddar
1 15-oz. can tomato sauce	cheese
1 tbsp. Worcestershire sauce	1 sm. loaf French or Italian
1 tsp. oregano	bread

Combine the soup mix, tomato sauce, Worcestershire sauce and oregano in a fondue pot and cook over medium heat for 5 to 10 minutes. Add the cheese, small amount at a time, and cook, stirring constantly, until cheese melts. Place on stand over burner. Cut the bread into cubes and dip bread cubes into cheese mixture. 8 servings.

Mrs. Dorothy Baker, Shreveport, Louisiana

FIRST-RATE WELSH RAREBIT

1 1/2 tbsp. butter or	1 c. milk
margarine	1/2 tsp. Worcestershire sauce
1 1/2 tbsp. flour	2 c. shredded sharp cheese
1 tsp. salt	Toast points or toasted
1/2 tsp. dry mustard	English muffins
1/8 tsp. paprika	

Melt the butter in a metal fondue pot over moderate flame. Stir in the flour, salt, mustard and paprika. Stir in the milk and Worcestershire sauce and cook, stirring constantly, until thickened. Add the cheese and cook, stirring constantly, until cheese is melted. Serve the rarebit on toast points. 6 servings.

Mrs. Jack Geffkin, Levelland, Texas

TOMATO-CHEESE FONDUE

1 can cream of tomato soup	**1 lb. Cheddar cheese,**
2/3 c. milk	**shredded**
2 tsp. prepared mustard	**1 tbsp. chopped chives (opt.)**

Combine first 3 ingredients in a fondue pot. Place over low flame and heat through, stirring frequently. Add the cheese, 1/2 cup at a time, and cook until cheese is melted. Stir in the chives. May serve with French bread cubes, small toast triangles or bread sticks. 6-8 servings.

Mrs. Richard Baker, Abilene, Texas

DOUBLE CHEESE FONDUE

1 10 3/4-oz. can Cheddar cheese soup	**1 med. clove of garlic, minced**
1 8-oz. package rectangular slices natural Swiss cheese	**French or Italian bread cubes**

Place the soup in a fondue pot. Cut the cheese in small pieces and add to soup. Add the garlic and place fondue pot over flame. Heat until cheese is melted, stirring occasionally. Spear bread with fondue fork or toothpick and dip into fondue.

Double Cheese Fondue (above)

Artichokes with Swiss Fondue (page 34)

vegetable fondues

Few things are more appetite-arousing than the sight of a plate heaped with gleaming fresh vegetables — carrots, beans, tomatoes, peppers, squash, and other garden-fresh and colorful vegetables. Now combine the delicious taste of vegetables with the fun of making fondues . . . try a vegetable fondue!

Mix and match bite-sized pieces of seasonal vegetables for your fondue fare. Cut carrots in half-inch slices . . . separate cauliflower into flowerets . . . stem, clean, and dry green beans . . . slice green or red peppers into half-inch lengthwise pieces . . . wash and dry zucchini and cut into half-inch pieces. Add fresh mushrooms and brilliant red cherry tomatoes, and you're ready for a delightful fondue.

Southern homemakers know that their region is famous for its many farm-fresh vegetables. They can turn that produce into delicious fondues, as the recipes on the following pages attest. And certainly the fun of spearing a vegetable chunk and cooking it in a fondue pot full of hot oil is so enchanting your entire family will be begging to eat vegetables!

For unusual taste treats and lots of laughter and good times, try a vegetable fondue using the very best of your region's vegetables — and the home-tested recipes in this section.

31

Vegetable Fondue Curry (below)

VEGETABLE FONDUE CURRY

1/4 c. butter	1 tsp. sugar
1 green onion, minced	4 whole cloves
2 tbsp. flour	Dash of cayenne pepper
1 tsp. minced gingerroot	2 c. milk
1/2 c. chopped apple	1/2 c. moist shredded coconut
1 to 2 tsp. curry powder	1/4 c. lemon juice
1 tsp. salt	Thin cream

Melt the butter in top of a double boiler over low heat. Add the onion and cook until transparent, stirring occasionally. Blend in the flour, then add the gingerroot, apple, curry powder, salt, sugar, cloves and cayenne pepper. Remove from heat and add the milk gradually. Cook, stirring constantly, until thickened. Place over simmering water and cover. Cook for 30 minutes. Remove the cloves and stir in the coconut. Add the lemon juice gradually. Pour into a fondue pot and place over low flame. Add cream if mixture becomes too thick. Serve with cauliflowerets, broccoli flowerets, zucchini and celery sticks, sliced carrots, green pepper and radishes and cherry tomatoes.

CAULIFLOWER-CHEESE FONDUE

1 tbsp. butter	1/2 tsp. salt
1/2 lb. Cheddar cheese, shredded	1 egg, separated
1/2 c. light cream	2 tbsp. cognac
1 tsp. Worcestershire sauce	Paprika to taste
3/4 tsp. horseradish	Cauliflowerets

Melt the butter in a fondue pot. Add the cheese, cream, Worcestershire sauce, horseradish and salt and cook, stirring, until cheese is melted. Stir small amount of cheese mixture into the beaten egg yolk, then stir back into cheese mixture. Cook for several minutes. Beat the egg white until stiff and fold into cheese mixture. Add the cognac and paprika. Place fondue pot over fondue burner. Place cauliflowerets on fondue forks and dip into fondue. 4-6 servings.

Mrs. Lindy Mann, Aiken, South Carolina

CAULIFLOWER SALAD FRITTERS

2 c. self-rising flour	Salt and pepper to taste
1/4 c. warm water	Cooked cauliflowerets
1 egg, beaten	1 chopped onion
2 tbsp. olive oil	1 tsp. chopped parsley
2 tsp. tarragon vinegar	

Combine the flour, water, egg and 1 tablespoon olive oil in a bowl and mix well. Let stand for at least 1 hour. Mix remaining oil, vinegar, salt and pepper in a deep bowl. Add the cauliflowerets, onion and parsley and let stand for 30 minutes, stirring occasionally. Drain the cauliflowerets and dip in batter. Fry in hot fat in a fondue pot or deep fat fryer until golden brown, then drain. May sprinkle cheese over fritters, if desired. Serve hot.

Mrs. Joyce MacBryde, Canton, North Carolina

CELERY IN SHRIMP FONDUE

1 8-oz. package cream cheese	1/2 c. sour cream
1 10-oz. can frozen cream of shrimp soup	1 tsp. prepared horseradish
	1/4 tsp. Worcestershire sauce
	Bite-sized pieces of celery

Heat the cream cheese in a saucepan until softened. Add the soup and cook, stirring, until blended. Add the sour cream, horseradish and Worcestershire sauce and heat through. Transfer to fondue pot and place over fondue burner. Dip celery pieces into sauce.

Mrs. John McCall, Columbia, South Carolina

33

ARTICHOKES WITH SWISS FONDUE

4 lge. artichokes	1 1/2 tsp. flour
1 1/8 tsp. salt	Dash of dry
3/4 c. dry white wine	mustard
1/2 lb. Swiss or Gruyere	Dash of nutmeg
cheese, grated	

Wash the artichokes. Cut off stems at base and remove small bottom leaves. Trim tips of leaves and cut off about 1 inch from top of artichokes, if desired. Stand artichokes upright in a deep saucepan large enough to hold snugly. Add 1 teaspoon salt and 2 to 3 inches boiling water and cover. Simmer for 35 to 45 minutes or until base may be pierced easily with a fork, adding more boiling water, if needed. Turn artichokes upside down to drain. Spread leaves apart gently and remove choke from center of artichokes with a metal spoon. Heat the wine to boiling point in a fondue pot or heavy enameled saucepan and reduce heat. Mix the cheese with remaining salt and remaining ingredients and stir into wine. Cook over medium heat, stirring, until smooth and thickened. Place over flame and keep hot. Dip artichoke leaves into fondue. 4 servings.

Photograph for this recipe on page 30.

CARROTS AND ARTICHOKE HEARTS FONDUE

2 lb. ripe tomatoes	1 tsp. powdered basil leaves
1 tbsp. cornstarch	Salt and pepper to taste
1/2 c. white wine	Carrot curls
3/4 lb. Swiss cheese, diced	Artichoke hearts, drained

Drop the tomatoes into boiling water briefly, then drain. Remove tomato skins. Cook the tomatoes in 2 cups water in a saucepan until soft. Mash through a sieve and discard seeds. Bring tomato puree to a boil in a fondue pot. Stir the cornstarch into wine. Add to tomato puree, stirring constantly, and cook until thickened. Stir in cheese and basil gradually and cook until cheese is melted. Place the fondue pot over a flame. Spear the carrot curls and artichoke hearts with fondue forks and dip into the fondue. 12 servings.

Mrs. Janet Cramer, Chickasha, Oklahoma

MUSHROOM FONDUE

1/2 lb. button mushrooms	1 tsp. salt
1 5-oz. can water chestnuts	1/4 tsp. pepper
Salad or peanut oil	Lemon Sauce
2 cloves of garlic, minced	

Wash and dry the mushrooms. Drain and dry the water chestnuts. Mix 1 cup oil, garlic, salt and pepper in a deep bowl. Add the mushrooms and water chestnuts and marinate for at least 1 hour. Drain the mushrooms and water chestnuts. Pour enough oil into a fondue pot to fill 1/2 full and heat to 360 degrees. Place the fondue pot over fondue burner. Spear the mushrooms and water chestnuts with fondue forks and cook in the oil to desired doneness. Dip into Lemon Sauce.

Lemon Sauce

1/2 c. butter	4 tbsp. lemon juice
3 egg yolks	1/4 tsp. salt

Divide the butter into 3 parts. Combine the egg yolks, lemon juice and 1 part butter in top of a double boiler and cook over hot water, stirring constantly with wire whisk, until butter melts. Add second part butter and cook until thickened. Add remaining butter and cook until butter has melted. Remove from heat and add the salt.

Mrs. Agnes Carr, Laurel, Maryland

CRISP EGGPLANT FONDUE

1 c. dry bread crumbs	1 c. peeled eggplant, cut
1/4 c. grated Parmesan	in cubes
cheese	1 egg, well beaten
Salt and pepper to taste	Salad oil

Combine the crumbs, cheese, salt and pepper in a bowl. Dip the eggplant cubes into beaten egg, then roll in crumb mixture. Pour enough oil into a fondue pot to fill to depth of 2 inches and heat to about 350 degrees. Spear eggplant cubes with fondue forks and fry in hot oil for 2 to 3 minutes or until golden brown. 6 servings.

Mrs. Joseph C. Pouncey, Chattanooga, Tennessee

ONION-BACON FONDUE

4 slices lean Canadian bacon	Nutmeg to taste
1/2 lb. Cheddar cheese,	Salt and pepper to taste
shredded	2 tbsp. applejack
2 tbsp. flour	2 loaves French bread
1 c. dry white wine	Sm. white onions, parboiled

Cut the bacon into small pieces. Mix the cheese with flour. Saute the bacon in a fondue pot until light brown. Pour in the wine and heat until wine begins to bubble. Add the cheese gradually and cook, stirring constantly, until cheese has melted. Season with nutmeg, salt and pepper. Add the applejack and heat through. Place on a stand over flame. Cut the bread into bite-sized pieces. Spear the bread and onions with fondue forks and dip into fondue.

Mrs. Sharon Harden, Hyattsville, Maryland

POTATO MARINES

2 servings instant mashed potatoes	Dash of white pepper
1 tsp. instant minced onion	1 7 1/2-oz. can crab meat
1 1/4 tsp. Worcestershire sauce	1 egg, lightly beaten
1/8 tsp. garlic powder	1/2 c. fine dry bread crumbs
	Salad oil

Prepare potatoes according to package directions, using 2 tablespoons less milk than called for and adding onion to water before boiling. Stir in the Worcestershire sauce, garlic powder and white pepper. Drain and flake the crab meat, then remove cartilage. Stir into potato mixture and shape into bite-sized balls. Dip into beaten egg, then roll in bread crumbs. Pour enough salad oil into fondue pot to fill 1/2 full and heat to 375 degrees. Place fondue pot over fondue burner. Spear potato balls with fondue forks. Fry in hot oil for 2 to 3 minutes.

Martha Jackson, Ashland, Kentucky

TINY POTATOES IN CURRY SAUCE

6 tbsp. butter or margarine	Salt and pepper to taste
2 tsp. curry powder	2 c. milk
4 tbsp. flour	2 doz. small cooked potatoes

Melt the butter in a saucepan. Stir in the curry and cook for 1 to 2 minutes. Blend in the flour, salt and pepper. Add the milk slowly and cook, stirring, until smooth and thick. Pour into a fondue pot and place over low flame. Place the potatoes on fondue forks and dip into sauce. Small, canned potatoes, drained, may be substituted for cooked potatoes.

Frances Rivers, Madison, Tennessee

TOMATO-PARMESAN FONDUE

1/2 lb. Gruyere cheese, shredded	2 tbsp. flour
1/4 lb. Parmesan cheese, shredded	2 c. dry white wine
	3 tbsp. kirsch
1/4 lb. Locatelli cheese, shredded	Nutmeg to taste
	Salt and pepper to taste
	Tomatoes, cut in wedges

Mix the cheeses with flour. Pour the wine into fondue pot and heat until wine begins to bubble. Stir in cheese gradually and cook, stirring constantly, until cheese has melted. Add the kirsch, nutmeg, salt and pepper. Place fondue pot on a stand over fondue burner. Place tomato wedges on fondue forks and dip into fondue.

Mrs. Jim West, Belle, West Virginia

FLAVOR-FULL GREEN BEANS

1 c. butter or margarine	Sm. whole green beans
1/3 c. olive or peanut oil	French bread, sliced thin
3 sm. garlic cloves, minced	

Combine first 3 ingredients in a metal fondue pot and heat over medium heat until bubbly. Place the fondue pot over a low flame. Spear the beans with fondue forks or long heavy bamboo skewers and swirl in butter mixture until hot and lightly browned. Hold a slice of bread under beans as removed from butter mixture.

Mrs. Jim Garvin, Arlington, Virginia

RINKTUM DITTY WITH BEANS

1 can tomato soup	Hot sauce to taste
2 c. shredded sharp Cheddar	1 egg, slightly beaten
cheese	2 c. cooked Great Northern
1/4 tsp. dry mustard	beans, drained
1/2 tsp. Worcestershire sauce	Salt and pepper to taste

Mix the soup, cheese, mustard, Worcestershire sauce and hot sauce in top of a double boiler and place over hot water. Cook, stirring frequently, until cheese is melted. Add the egg quickly and cook, stirring constantly, until smooth. Stir in the beans, salt and pepper and heat through. Place in a fondue pot and place over a flame. Serve with hot, buttered toast. 6-8 servings.

Rinktum Ditty with Beans (above)

37

fondue beverages, sauces and desserts

Dessert fondues are the brainchild of a New York public relations woman — but southern women have developed very special kinds of recipes to create dessert fondues uniquely their own. You'll find the very best of these recipes in the pages that follow. These are the dessert fondues served in homes from Maryland to Texas when something extra-special is wanted to cap a meal.

You, your family, and your guests will also delight in dessert fondues. The one most frequently served is chocolate which has been melted into a rich, fudgy goodness. Mouth-watering tidbits — fruit chunks, ladyfingers, champagne biscuits, tiny doughnuts, or sweet cookies — are speared with a fondue fork and dipped into the sauce.

For special treats, cut fresh fruit into chunks or wedges. Then put the pieces in a single layer, cover with waxed paper or plastic wrap, and freeze for two hours before serving. Remove from the freezer for ten minutes, then carry the beautifully frosted fruit to your eager diners. As they dip the fruit pieces in the fondue pot, the hot chocolate sauce will coat the iced fruit, turning it into a candy-like confection!

In addition to elegantly delicious dessert fondue recipes, this section brings you sauce and beverage recipes to complement every course and every kind of fondue meal. In fact, this section is just what you need to finish your meals with that certain flair that marks a great cook!

39

APPLE FONDUE BEVERAGE

1 qt. apple cider or **apple juice**	**2 tbsp. red cinnamon** **candies**

Combine the cider and cinnamon candies in a fondue pot and stir over medium flame until candies are dissolved and cider is hot. Pour into mugs. Garnish each serving with an unpeeled apple slice and cinnamon stick, if desired. 6-8 servings.

Mrs. D. R. Russell, Greeneville, Tennessee

AT-THE-TABLE HOT CHOCOLATE

2 1/2 c. milk	**1/2 c. semisweet or milk chocolate bits**
1 tbsp. sugar	**1 tsp. vanilla**
Dash of salt	**Marshmallows (opt.)**

Scald the milk in a metal fondue pot over moderate flame and add the sugar and salt. Add the chocolate bits, small amount at a time, and stir until melted. Heat to desired serving temperature, stirring frequently, and stir in vanilla. Ladle into cups and top with marshmallows. 4 servings.

Janet Slater, Fairmont, West Virginia

FONDUE CAFE

2 tbsp. sugar	**2 sm. cinnamon sticks,**
1 tsp. grated orange rind	**broken in half**
4 whole cloves	**4 c. strong hot black coffee**
3 tbsp. brandy extract	

Combine first 5 ingredients in a metal fondue pot and place over a low flame. Add the coffee gradually, stirring constantly. Ladle into demitasse cups at once. 8-10 servings.

Mrs. Luther Manning, Meridian, Mississippi

JAMAICAN BLAZER

3 c. boiling water	**1/2 tsp. butter**
1 can concentrated pineapple **juice**	**Dash of angostura bitters** **6 whole cloves**

Pour the boiling water into a large, metal fondue pot over high flame and bring to a boil. Lower the flame and stir in remaining ingredients. Bring to a boil, then remove from heat. Let stand for 2 to 3 minutes. Ladle into heavy mugs. 3-4 servings.

Tina Livingston, North Little Rock, Arkansas

MULLED CHERRY PUNCH

1 sm. cinnamon stick, broken
   in pieces
1/4 tsp. ground cloves
1/4 tsp. nutmeg
1/4 c. lemon juice

2/3 c. sugar
1 1-qt. bottle cherry soda
1 c. maraschino cherries
Thin lemon slices

Combine all ingredients except lemon slices in a metal fondue pot and place over a moderate flame. Heat to serving temperature. Ladle into small mugs or punch cups and top each serving with a lemon slice. 8 servings.

Mrs. A. A. Kelton, Baton Rouge, Louisiana

WASSAIL BOWL

1/2 c. sugar
1/2 c. water
12 whole cloves
2 2-in. pieces of stick
   cinnamon
1 1/2 qt. orange juice

2 c. grapefruit juice
1 qt. sweet cider
1 orange
Candied cherries
Angelica

Combine the sugar, water and spices in a deep saucepan and simmer for 10 minutes. Strain. Add the orange juice, grapefruit juice and cider and heat through. Pour into a fondue pot and keep hot. Slice the orange. Place a halved candied cherry in center of each slice and place pieces of angelica, cut to resemble holly leaves, on both sides of cherry. Float slices on top of punch. 25 1/2-cup servings.

Wassail Bowl (above)

RANGE APPLE CIDER

6 c. cider or apple juice
2 sm. cinnamon sticks
8 to 10 whole cloves

1/4 tsp. grated orange rind
Orange slices

Combine all ingredients except orange slices in a metal fondue pot and place over a moderate flame. Heat to serving temperature. Ladle into mugs and top each serving with an orange slice. 6 servings.

Mrs. Ralph Wagner, Valdosta, Georgia

RUSSIAN TEA

1 c. sugar
1 3-in. stick cinnamon
1 12-oz. can pineapple
   juice

Juice and rind of 3 oranges
Juice and rind of 2 lemons
4 tsp. tea leaves

Mix the sugar, 1 cup water and cinnamon in a large fondue pot and bring to a boil. Boil for 5 minutes, then remove the cinnamon. Add the pineapple juice, orange juice, lemon juice and 4 cups water. Place the orange and lemon rinds in a saucepan and add 2 cups water. Bring to a boil and boil for 3 minutes. Strain and add the liquid to juice mixture. Pour 1 cup boiling water over the tea and cover. Steep for 3 minutes, then strain and discard leaves. Add tea to juice mixture and bring to a boil. Place the fondue pot over fondue burner. Ladle into cups and garnish each serving with a lemon slice, if desired. 14 servings.

Catherine Thomas, Dyer, Tennessee

CARAMEL-NUT SAUCE

1 c. (packed) brown sugar
1/2 c. light corn syrup
1/4 c. water
1 tsp. cornstarch

Dash of salt
1/2 c. chopped pecans
1 tbsp. butter or margarine

Combine first 5 ingredients in a metal fondue pot and mix. Place on fondue stand over high flame and cook, stirring constantly, until sauce thickens and clears. Stir in the pecans and butter. Lower flame and keep warm. Ladle over sliced cake, waffles or ice cream.

Verna Tracy, Broken Bow, Oklahoma

GOURMET CRANBERRY SAUCE

2 tbsp. cornstarch
3 tbsp. water
1 1/2 c. whole cranberry sauce

1/2 tsp. grated orange rind
1/4 c. brandy

Mix the cornstarch and water. Add remaining ingredients except brandy and pour into a metal fondue pot. Place over a moderate flame and stir constantly until thickened. Stir in the brandy. Serve warm on waffles or ice cream.

Mrs. Claude Swift, Charlotte, North Carolina

HAWAIIAN SUNDAE SAUCE

1   8 1/2-oz. can crushed
    pineapple
3/4 c. light corn syrup
3 tbsp. sugar

Dash of salt
1 tbsp. grated orange
   rind (opt.)

Drain the pineapple and reserve juice. Combine reserved juice, corn syrup, sugar and salt in a metal fondue pot. Place on a stand over high flame and stir until sugar dissolves. Cook over low flame for about 10 minutes or until thick, stirring frequently. Stir in pineapple and orange rind and serve on ice cream, pancakes or waffles.

Amelia Lane, West Columbia, South Carolina

INDIENNE SPICED HONEY

1/2 c. butter or margarine
1/4 tsp. cinnamon

1/8 tsp. nutmeg
1/2 c. honey

Melt the butter in a metal fondue pot over high flame. Stir in the spices and honey and heat through. Remove pot from flame and stir vigorously until blended. Lower flame and place fondue pot over flame. Ladle over hot cakes or waffles.

Mrs. Everette Glynn, Fredricksburg, Virginia

ORANGE-MAPLE SUCRE

1/4 c. butter or margarine
1 tbsp. flour
1/4 c. (packed) light brown
   sugar
1/4 c. water

1/4 c. maple-flavored
   pancake syrup
1/4 c. orange juice
1 tsp. grated orange rind
2 tbsp. sherry (opt.)

Melt the butter in a metal fondue pot over flame. Stir in the flour and sugar and heat until bubbly. Stir in remaining ingredients except sherry and simmer for 2 to 3 minutes. Stir in the sherry and ladle over pancakes or waffles.

Mrs. George Trout, Dover, Delaware

Peaches Chantilly with Sauce (below)

PEACHES CHANTILLY WITH SAUCE

8 peach halves	1/2 c. raspberry jelly
Vanilla ice cream	8 tbsp. orange-flavored
Whipped cream	liqueur

Arrange the peach halves and ice cream in 4 sherbet glasses. Top with whipped cream and place in freezer. Melt the raspberry jelly in a small fondue pot over a flame. Blend in 6 tablespoons orange-flavored liqueur and heat until bubbly. Heat remaining liqueur in a large serving spoon over flame. Ignite and stir into raspberry sauce. Ladle over peaches and ice cream. Serve with wafers, if desired. 4 servings.

BUTTERSCOTCH DESSERT FONDUE

1/2 c. butter or margarine	1 can sweetened condensed milk
2 c. brown sugar	1 tsp. vanilla
1 c. light corn syrup	Pound cake cubes

Melt the butter in a saucepan. Stir in the sugar, corn syrup and 2 tablespoons water and bring to boiling point. Stir in the milk and simmer, stirring constantly, until mixture reaches to 230 degrees on a candy thermometer or thread stage. Add the vanilla. Pour into a fondue pot and place over fondue burner. Spear cake cubes with fondue fork and dip in fondue. Add small amount of milk or water if fondue becomes too thick. Vanilla wafers, apple cubes or popcorn may be substituted for pound cake.

Mrs. Taylor Henderson, Hammond, Louisiana

SPICED WINTER APPLESAUCE

1 16-oz. can applesauce	1/2 tsp. cinnamon
1/2 c. maple-flavored	Dash of cloves
pancake syrup	

Combine all ingredients in a metal fondue pot and heat over high flame, stirring frequently. Lower flame and keep warm. Ladle onto potato pancakes or waffles.

Mrs. Viola Walker, Manchester, Kentucky

ORANGE-HONEY SAUCE

1/4 c. butter or margarine	1/2 c. thick orange
1/2 c. honey	marmalade

Melt the butter in a metal fondue pot over high flame. Stir in the honey and marmalade and heat through. Lower the flame and keep warm. Ladle over hot cakes or waffles.

Mrs. Dennis Carlisle, Hagerstown, Maryland

FRIED FRUIT PIES

1 10-oz. package pie	Cooking oil
crust mix	Confectioners' sugar
Canned fruit pie filling	

Prepare pie crust according to package directions and shape into a ball. Wrap in aluminum foil or waxed paper and chill for 15 to 20 minutes. Roll out on a floured board to 1/8-inch thickness and cut into 2 3/4-inch rounds with floured cookie cutter. Spoon 1 teaspoon filling on one side of each pastry round. Moisten edges and fold pastry in half. Seal and flute edges with fork. Place on a tray and cover. Chill. Fill a metal fondue pot 1/2 full with oil and heat to 350 degrees. Place on stand over high flame. Place pie on fondue fork or bamboo skewer and lower into hot oil. Cook for about 5 minutes or until lightly browned. Remove from fork and dust with confectioners' sugar. Cool slightly before serving.

Mrs. Jane Blount, Chattanooga, Tennessee

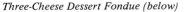
Three-Cheese Dessert Fondue (below)

THREE-CHEESE DESSERT FONDUE

1 3-oz. package cream cheese	1 tbsp. flour
3/4 c. grated Cheddar cheese	1/2 c. white wine
3/4 c. grated Swiss cheese	1/8 tsp. garlic salt
	Dash of cayenne pepper

Pour 1 cup water into fondue base and position tray, rack and bowl. Cut the cream cheese in cubes. Mix the cheeses with flour. Plug unit into outlet. Pour the wine into fondue bowl and heat until bubbles rise to surface. Stir in cheeses, small amount at a time, and heat, stirring, until melted. Beat with fork to blend smoothly. Stir in garlic salt and cayenne pepper. Use wedges of fresh pears and apples for dippers. 1 1/2 cups.

FRUITY FRITTERS

1 c. sifted flour	1 tbsp. melted butter or
3 tbsp. sugar	margarine
1 1/2 tsp. baking powder	Cooking oil
1/2 tsp. salt	Bananas
2 eggs, beaten	Confectioners' sugar
1/3 c. milk	

Combine first 4 ingredients and sift into a bowl. Add the eggs, milk and butter and stir until smooth. Fill metal fondue pot 1/2 full with oil and heat to 350 degrees. Place pot on stand over fondue burner. Cut bananas crosswise into 1-inch slices. Spear banana slice with fondue fork and dip into batter. Drain. Cook in hot oil until golden brown. Cool slightly, then roll in confectioners' sugar. Whole fresh strawberries may be substituted for banana slices.

Melba Colvin, Opp, Alabama

BANANA SCALLOPS

1 egg, lightly beaten	6 firm bananas, sliced 1 in. thick
1 1/2 tsp. salt	3/4 c. fine cereal crumbs

Mix the egg and salt. Dip bananas into egg mixture, then roll in crumbs. Fry in hot, deep fat in a fondue pot for about 2 minutes or until brown and tender. Drain and serve immediately.

Mrs. William Shaw, Camden, Arkansas

STRAWBERRY FONDUE

1 4-oz. carton whipped cream cheese	1/4 c. cornstarch
2 10-oz. packages frozen strawberries, thawed	2 tbsp. sugar
	1/4 c. brandy

Let cream cheese come to room temperature. Crush the strawberries in a saucepan. Mix the cornstarch and 1/2 cup cold water and stir into the strawberries. Cook and stir until thickened. Sieve and discard seeds. Pour strawberry puree into a fondue pot and place over fondue burner. Add the cream cheese and stir until melted. Stir in the sugar and add the brandy gradually. Spear pear or peach cubes or pound cake cubes with fondue fork and dip into fondue.

Mrs. Henry Welch, Brownwood, Texas

MINTED FONDUE

1/2 c. milk	3/4 c. finely crushed peppermint candies
3 tbsp. butter or margarine	2 drops of red food coloring
1 14-oz. package creamy white frosting mix	

Heat the milk and butter in a saucepan until the butter is melted. Add the frosting mix and peppermint candies and mix well. Stir in the food coloring. Pour into a fondue pot and place over fondue burner. Dip chocolate wafers, pound cake cubes or angel cake cubes into fondue.

Mrs. Norton Slayton, Clovis, New Mexico

PEACH-CHOCOLATE FONDUE

1 1-lb. 13-oz. can cling peach slices	2 tbsp. butter
1 6-oz. package chocolate bits	1/4 c. orange juice
	1 tbsp. grated orange rind

Drain the peaches. Combine the chocolate bits, butter, orange juice and grated rind in a fondue pot and place over low heat. Stir until chocolate is melted. Keep warm over flame. Dip peaches in fondue. 6 servings.

Photograph for this recipe on page 38.

TANGY ORANGE FONDUE

3 tbsp. butter or margarine	1/3 c. orange marmalade
3 tbsp. sugar	1/2 tsp. grated orange rind
1 tbsp. flour	
1/2 c. heavy cream	

Melt the butter in a fondue pot over low flame. Mix the sugar and flour and stir into butter. Stir in the cream and cook, stirring frequently, until thickened. Stir in marmalade and orange rind. Spear pineapple or banana chunks with fondue forks or bamboo skewers and dip into fondue.

Mrs. Inez Robbins, Columbus, Georgia

CHOCOLATE FONDUE

2 tbsp. honey or light corn syrup	1 9-oz. bar milk chocolate
1/2 c. light cream or half and half	1/4 c. finely chopped pecans
	1 tsp. vanilla

Heat the honey and cream in a fondue pot over flame. Break the chocolate in small pieces and add to honey mixture. Heat, stirring constantly, until chocolate is melted. Stir in pecans and vanilla. Place bite-sized pieces of cake or miniature marshmallows on fondue forks and twirl in chocolate mixture. Cool slightly.

Mrs. Yvonne Ayers, Bradenton, Florida

CHOCOLATE-MARSHMALLOW FONDUE

1/8 tsp. cinnamon	12 oz. sweet cooking chocolate
1 tsp. sugar	1/2 c. miniature marshmallows
3/4 c. heavy cream	2 tbsp. brandy

Mix the cinnamon and sugar in a 2-cup fondue pot and blend in the cream. Add the chocolate and cook over very low heat, stirring frequently, until chocolate melts and mixture is smooth. Add the marshmallows and stir until melted. Stir in the brandy. Place fondue pot on stand over very low heat. Place stemmed red maraschino cherries, chunks of ripe fruit or chunks of pound cake or angel food cake on fondue forks and dip into fondue.

Photograph for this recipe on page 2.

CHOCOLATE FONDUE MARVEILLEUSE

1 12-oz. package semisweet chocolates	Pinch of salt
2 cans sweetened condensed milk	Vanilla, almond flavoring or brandy flavoring to taste

Mix the chocolates, milk, salt and vanilla in a fondue pot and place over burner. Heat, stirring frequently, until chocolates are melted. Keep warm. Place marshmallows, doughnut pieces and banana slices on fondue forks and dip into fondue.

Chocolate Fondue Marveilleuse (above)

chafing dish cookery

Cooking foods in a chafing dish is one of the oldest and most elegant ways of preparing recipes. The forerunner of the modern chafing dish was the tri-legged brazier, standard equipment in ancient homes from Babylon to Egypt.

It was a Frenchman — Alexis Soger — who in the 19th century streamlined the brazier and gave it a combined double-boiler and frying pan construction. His innovation ushered in the golden age of chafing dish cookery. Hostesses created elegant masterpieces in front of their admiring guests. This custom of chafing dish cookery at parties has continued. Even today, the rush of modern life has not displaced the chafing dish from its place as the epitome of elegant dining.

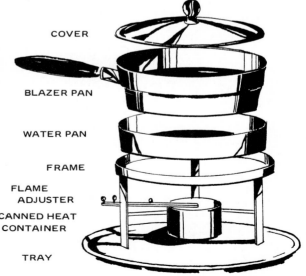

COVER

BLAZER PAN

WATER PAN

FRAME

FLAME ADJUSTER

CANNED HEAT CONTAINER

TRAY

Chafing dishes come in sizes ranging from the very small ones used to prepare dessert sauces or party appetizers to the three-quart sizes which hold a main dish for many people. And they come in a variety of materials: sterling silver, copper, brass, stainless steel, and plain or color-coated aluminum. Those made of silver-plate or copper-plate will need replating from time to time; those made of other materials are highly durable.

The traditional chafing dish has a cover, a top pan called the blazer, a bottom pan known as the bain-marie (from the French word for water bath) which holds hot water, a stand, a burner with flame adjuster, and a heat-proof tray. The blazer pan can be used over direct heat as a frying pan and then placed over the bain-marie to keep the food warm. Some chafing dish recipes are prepared in the kitchen, then brought to the table and kept warm in the blazer pan over the bain-marie.

There are many other pans which can be used to bring variety to your chafing dish cookery. Among them are the *round crepes/omelet pan,* usually 13 to 14 inches in diameter and one inch deep; the *crepes suzette* pan, similar to the skillet but only 1" to 1 1/2" deep; and the *oval-shaped omelet, fish, or frying pan* which is 11" to 13" long, 5" to 7" wide, and 1" to 1 1/2" deep.

The chafing dish has its own *heat source:* an alcohol lamp or burner, electricity, or canned heat. Some chafing dishes have candle warmers, but these do not cook food — they only keep it warm. Alcohol and canned heat are discussed in detail on pages 6 to 7.

What can you cook in a chafing dish? Not everything. Complicated dishes . . . those with long cooking times . . . and large quantities of food are best cooked in the kitchen and served from chafing dishes. When you are considering a recipe for chafing dish cookery, choose a simple one that cooks quickly. Foods such as dessert sauces . . . party appetizers . . . main dishes featuring small pieces of meat, shrimp, or other seafood are all ideal for chafing dish cookery.

When you are planning to cook in your chafing dish at the table, all food preparation should be done prior to the actual cooking. Foods should be chopped, diced, or mixed if that is what the recipe specifies. Each individual food or group of seasonings should be carefully measured and placed in individual dishes. These dishes go onto an attractive serving tray along with any utensils you may need. Try to use wooden utensils: metal ones may scratch the surface of your chafing dish.

Before using the chafing dish, remove the cover, blazer pan, and bain-marie from the frame. Place the chafing dish stand onto the tray which comes with it. Set the fuel in place. If your recipe specifies that you cook over the bain-marie, set it firmly into the stand and fill it one-quarter to one-half full of hot water.

You will always do your cooking in the blazer pan, which is placed either directly over the heat source or over the bain-marie. Add ingredients in small amounts and let them warm throughout before adding more.

When cleaning the chafing dish, let it cool completely to prevent discoloration or warping during washing. Empty the fuel container. If possible, remove handles and knobs; if this cannot be done, avoid wetting them. Do not soak a chafing dish as it may stain or streak the finish.

chafing dish appetizers

At every party, the guests inevitably head for a table or tray which holds appetizers — those tiny tidbits of food so important to the success of any gathering. And when they see hot appetizers, your guests immediately know that your party is going to feature some of the most delicious appetizers ever.

Yes, serving hot appetizers is an unmistakable sign of true hospitality. Southern hostesses know this, and they depend on their chafing dishes to keep hot appetizers at the peak of their flavor goodness for hours. Somehow just the sight of a chafing dish with its candle warmer briskly burning signals to all present that something delicious is waiting inside.

And something delicious is waiting inside the pages of the following section — mouth-watering, home-tested appetizer recipes just made to be served from your chafing dish. For a spectacular but easy appetizer, try serving Cocktail Almonds. Another exciting party dish comes to your table when you serve lively-flavored Sweet and Sour Meatballs. Speared with brightly-decorated cocktail toothpicks, these tiny meatballs are a treat certain to be enjoyed by all.

These are just two of the many party-perfect recipes you'll discover in this section. To highlight your skill as a clever hostess, serve chafing dish appetizers. They turn the simplest gathering into a gala occasion.

53

BEAN AND BACON DIP

1 can bean and bacon soup
1/4 c. chili sauce or catsup
2 tbsp. minced green pepper

Dash of onion salt
1 tsp. Worcestershire sauce

Mix all ingredients in a saucepan and bring to a boil. Simmer until thick, then place in a chafing dish. Keep hot over water. Serve with toast rounds, if desired.

Mrs. Harold F. Maxon, Buckhannon, West Virginia

CALIENTE SAUCE

2 cans refried beans
2 tbsp. chopped jalapeno
peppers
1/2 tsp. jalapeno pepper
liquid

1 tsp. Worcestershire sauce
6 tbsp. melted margarine
Instant minced onion to taste
Garlic salt to taste

Mix all ingredients in a chafing dish and heat through. Place over hot water and serve with corn chips, crackers or tostados. 12-16 servings.

Mrs. Imogene Spring, Seymour, Texas

CHEESE DIABLO

1   8-oz. package cream
cheese
1   4 1/2-oz. can deviled ham

3 tbsp. milk
1 tbsp. finely chopped onion
1 tbsp. chopped pimento

Melt the cream cheese in blazer pan of chafing dish over low heat, stirring constantly. Add the deviled ham, milk, onion and pimento and heat through. Place the blazer pan over water pan and keep warm. Serve with round buttery crackers and crisp vegetables. 1 1/2 cups.

Mrs. F. S. Oglesby, Winter Haven, Florida

SMOKY BACON DIP

1   8-oz. package cream
cheese
2 c. shredded American
process cheese
1/2 c. milk

1/4 tsp. onion salt
1/4 tsp. dry mustard
3 drops of hot sauce
6 slices cooked smoked
bacon, crumbled

Melt the cream cheese in blazer pan of small chafing dish over low heat, stirring constantly. Add the American cheese, milk, onion salt, mustard and hot sauce and cook, stirring constantly, until cheeses melt. Add the bacon and keep warm over hot water. Serve with assorted crackers. Stir in additional milk if mixture becomes too thick. 1 1/2 cups.

Mrs. Wayne Polk, Chapel Hill, North Carolina

COCHEESE CHILI DIP

1   15-oz. can chili with
    beans
1   10-oz. package frozen
    Welsh rarebit

1 tsp. Worcestershire sauce
1/4 tsp. garlic powder
Hot sauce to taste

Pour the chili with beans into blazer pan of chafing dish and mash beans with fork. Add the Welsh rarebit, Worcestershire sauce, garlic powder and hot sauce and cook over moderate heat, stirring constantly, until blended and heated through. Place blazer pan over water pan and keep warm. Serve with corn chips. 3 cups.

Sherry Townsend, Holbrook, Arizona

WELSH RAREBIT

1/4 c. butter
8 c. shredded sharp Cheddar
    cheese
2 tsp. Worcestershire sauce

1 tsp. dry mustard
Dash of cayenne pepper
1 c. light cream
4 eggs, slightly beaten

Melt the butter in a blazer pan or top of double boiler over hot water. Add the cheese and heat, stirring occasionally, until cheese is melted. Stir in the Worcestershire sauce, mustard and cayenne pepper. Combine the cream and eggs and stir into cheese mixture. Cook until thick, stirring frequently. Keep warm. Serve over buttered English muffins or buttered toast triangles, hard-cooked egg slices, broiled mushroom caps stuffed with cooked, crumbled bacon, shrimp, crab meat, asparagus spears and tomato slices.

Welsh Rarebit (above)

GARLIC-CHEESE-CLAM DIP

1 7 1/2-oz. can minced clams	1 1/2 tsp. Worcestershire sauce
1 8-oz. package cream cheese	1/2 tsp. lemon juice
1 clove of garlic, crushed	1/4 tsp. paprika

Drain the clams, reserving 2 teaspoons juice. Melt the cream cheese in blazer pan of chafing dish over low heat, stirring constantly. Add the clams, reserved juice, garlic, Worcestershire sauce, lemon juice and paprika and cook, stirring constantly, until blended and heated through. Place blazer pan over water pan and keep warm. Serve with assorted crackers, chips, or celery sticks. 1 cup.

Mrs. Chester Miller, Springer, New Mexico

MEXICAN CHEESE

2 sm. cans green chili peppers	1/2 lb. grated Cheddar cheese
1 1-lb. 13-oz. can stewed tomatoes	1/2 lb. grated Velveeta cheese
1 med. onion, chopped	

Drain and chop the chili peppers. Place in a saucepan. Add the tomatoes and onion and cook until thick. Add cheeses and cook over low heat until cheeses melt. Place in a chafing dish over hot water and serve with chips or crackers.

Mrs. Joanne Shirer, El Paso, Texas

ONION FROMAGE

2 tbsp. butter or margarine	1 1/3 c. boiling water
3 tbsp. all-purpose flour	1 c. shredded process cheese spread
2 tsp. grated onion	1 c. shredded Swiss process cheese
1/4 tsp. hot sauce	
Dash of pepper	
1 beef bouillon cube	

Melt the butter in blazer pan of chafing dish over low heat, then blend in the flour, onion, hot sauce and pepper. Dissolve the bouillon cube in boiling water and add to flour mixture. Cook, stirring constantly, until thickened. Add the cheeses and heat, stirring constantly, until melted. Place blazer pan over water pan and keep warm. Serve with ham cubes, garlic bread sticks, rye melba toast or rye crackers. 2 cups.

Lucy Locklin, Tulsa, Oklahoma

COCKTAIL ALMONDS

1 lb. almonds, skins removed	1/4 c. butter or oil
	1/4 c. salt

Preheat oven to 250 degrees. Blanch the almonds in boiling water for 1 minute. Drain and spread on a cookie sheet. Bake until dry. Heat the butter in blazer pan of chafing dish. Add the almonds and cook over low heat until golden. Sprinkle with salt and place blazer pan over hot water. 4 servings.

Mrs. B. N. Payne, Spartanburg, South Carolina

POLYNESIAN CHAFING DISH MEATS

2 tbsp. cornstarch
2 tbsp. sugar
1 chicken bouillon cube
1 c. pineapple juice
1/3 c. vinegar
2 tbsp. soy sauce
1 tbsp. butter or margarine

1/2 lb. tiny beef balls, cooked
1/2 lb. cooked shrimp, peeled
1/2 lb. chicken livers, cooked and halved

Combine first 3 ingredients in blazer pan of chafing dish. Add the pineapple juice, 1/2 cup water, vinegar, soy sauce and butter and bring to a boil over low heat, stirring constantly. Cover and simmer for 5 minutes. Place the beef balls, shrimp and livers in sauce and heat through. Keep warm over hot water. Spear meats with cocktail picks to serve. 60-65 appetizers.

Mrs. Julian Neeley, Wilmington, Delaware

BACON ROLL-UPS

8 slices bread, crusts removed
12 slices bacon, halved

Grated Parmesan cheese
24 stuffed green olives

Preheat oven to 350 degrees. Cut bread slices into 3 strips each. Place 1 bread strip on 1/2 slice bacon and sprinkle with cheese. Place an olive at 1 end and roll up. Secure with toothpick and place in shallow baking pan. Bake for 20 to 30 minutes. Place in a chafing dish and keep hot. 24 rolls.

Mrs. Robert Pruitt, Madisonville, Tennessee

BROILED CHICKEN LIVERS

Sliced bacon
Water chestnuts

Soy sauce
Chicken livers

Cut the bacon strips in half and quarter the water chestnuts. Marinate bacon and water chestnuts in soy sauce for at least 1 hour, then drain. Cut the chicken livers in small pieces. Wrap 1 piece of chicken liver and 1 piece of water chestnut with bacon strip and secure with toothpick. Place in a shallow baking pan. Broil until bacon is browned. Place in a chafing dish and keep warm.

Mrs. Louie B. Nunn, Frankfort, Kentucky

SWEET AND SOUR MEATBALLS

2 lb. ground beef	Garlic salt to taste
2 eggs	1 bottle chili sauce
1/2 c. cracker crumbs	1/2 c. grape jelly
1/2 c. water	Juice of 1 lemon
Salt and pepper to taste	

Mix the ground beef, eggs, cracker crumbs, water, salt, pepper and garlic salt and shape into small meatballs. Mix remaining ingredients in a blazer pan and heat through. Place meatballs in sauce and cover. Simmer for 5 to 10 minutes. Place the blazer pan over water pan and place over low flame. 48 meatballs.

Mrs. Henry Gunter, Williamsburg, Kentucky

CHAFING DISH SAUSAGES ITALIANO

2 8-oz. packages smoked brown-and-serve sausage links	1 env. spaghetti sauce mix
	1 1/4 c. water

Cut the sausage links in thirds crosswise. Prepare spaghetti sauce mix according to package directions, using canned tomato sauce variation and substituting 1 1/4 cups water for the recommended amount. Pour into blazer pan of chafing dish. Add sausage and heat through over low heat. Keep warm over hot water. Spear with cocktail picks to serve. About 65 appetizers.

Mrs. Carl Newton, Jackson, Mississippi

CHICKEN AND OYSTERS A LA KING

1 10-oz. can frozen oysters	3 c. milk
6 tbsp. butter	1 4-oz. can sliced mushrooms
1/2 c. chopped onion	1 egg, beaten
1/2 c. chopped celery	3 c. chopped cooked chicken
1/2 c. chopped green pepper	1 1/2 tbsp. chopped pimento
2/3 c. all-purpose flour	Softened butter
1 tsp. salt	8 lge. English muffins, split
1/8 tsp. pepper	Grated Parmesan cheese

Thaw the oysters. Drain and reserve 1/2 cup liquid. Melt the butter in a 3-quart saucepan. Add the onion, celery and green pepper and saute until tender. Stir in the flour, salt and pepper. Remove from heat and stir in milk and reserved oyster liquid gradually. Add the oysters and mushrooms and liquid and cook over medium heat, stirring constantly, until thickened. Blend small amount of hot mixture into egg, then stir back into hot mixture. Cook for 1 minute. Add chicken and pimento and cover. Heat over low heat to serving temperature. Do not boil. Place in a chafing dish and keep warm. Butter muffins and sprinkle with Parmesan cheese. Toast under broiler. Serve chicken mixture over English muffins. One pint fresh oysters may be substituted for frozen oysters.

CHICKEN IN CANAPE SHELLS

Pastry for 2-crust pie
1 6-oz. can broiled mushrooms
2 5-oz. cans boned chicken
1/2 c. finely diced celery
2/3 c. sour cream

1 tsp. grated onion
1/2 tsp. curry powder
1/2 tsp. salt
Cherry tomatoes, sliced
Parsley sprigs

Divide the pastry in half and roll each half to 12-inch round on lightly floured board. Cut into rounds with 1 3/4-inch scalloped cutter. Fit into tiny muffin pan cups and prick pastry with fork. Bake at 425 degrees for 7 minutes, then cool on wire racks. Drain the mushrooms and chop fine. Chop the chicken. Combine the mushrooms with chicken and celery in a blazer pan. Mix the sour cream, onion, curry powder and salt. Add to the chicken mixture and mix well. Place blazer pan over water pan and keep warm. Spoon 1 rounded teaspoon chicken mixture into each canape shell just before serving and garnish with tomato slices and parsley.

Mrs. Thomas G. Fulton, Aberdeen, Maryland

SAVORY CHESTNUTS

Chicken livers, partially cooked
Barbecue sauce

Bacon strips
Canned Chinese chestnuts, drained

Marinate the chicken livers in barbecue sauce for about 1 hour, then drain. Wrap each bacon strip around 1 chicken liver and 1 Chinese chestnut and fasten with toothpick. Place in a cookie pan. Broil until bacon is crisp. Place in a chafing dish and keep hot.

Mrs. John Hull, Rockville, Maryland

Chicken and Oysters a la King (page 58)

POISSON A COQUILLES IN WINE

1 1-lb. package frozen
scallops
1/2 lb. cooked shrimp
1/2 c. dry white wine
1/4 c. salad oil
2 tsp. minced onion
1 tsp. sugar

1/4 tsp. salt
Dash of dried rosemary
leaves, crushed
Dash of pepper
2 tbsp. melted butter or
margarine
1 tbsp. lemon juice

Cook the scallops according to package directions, then cool. Cut the scallops and shrimp into bite-sized pieces and place in a bowl. Combine the wine, oil, onion, sugar, salt, rosemary and pepper and pour over seafood. Marinate for several hours in refrigerator, stirring occasionally. Drain the seafood, reserving marinade. Place seafood in blazer pan of chafing dish. Combine the marinade, butter and lemon juice and pour over seafood. Heat through over low heat. Keep warm over hot water. 50 appetizers.

Mrs. Greg Whitley, Albuquerque, New Mexico

GULF SHRIMP DIP

1 10-oz. can frozen cream
of shrimp soup
1 c. shredded American
process cheese

1/2 lb. boiled shrimp,
chopped
1/4 c. milk
1/4 tsp. hot sauce

Combine all ingredients in blazer pan of chafing dish. Heat over low heat, stirring, until bubbly. Keep warm over hot water. Serve with melba toast. 2 1/4 cups.

Mrs. Wes Cranford, Fort Worth, Texas

ROCK LOBSTER APPETIZERS

12 2-oz. frozen rock
lobster-tails
6 tbsp. butter or margarine
6 tbsp. flour
1 1/2 c. light cream
1 tsp. grated lemon rind

1 tsp. paprika
2 eggs, separated
Salt and pepper to taste
1/2 c. grated Cheddar or
Parmesan cheese

Drop frozen rock lobster-tails into boiling, salted water and bring to a boil. Drain lobster-tails immediately and drench with cold water. Remove underside membrane with scissors and pull out meat. Dice the meat and reserve shells. Melt the butter in a saucepan and stir in flour. Stir in the cream gradually and add lemon rind and paprika. Cook, stirring constantly, until thickened. Beat in egg yolks quickly and add salt and pepper. Add lobster meat to half the sauce and spoon into reserved shells. Place in a cookie pan. Heat remaining sauce and stir in the cheese until melted. Cool slightly and fold in the stiffly beaten egg whites. Spoon over filled lobster shells. Bake in a 350-degree oven for 25 to 30 minutes or until puffed and brown. Place in chafing dish to keep warm. 6 servings.

Photograph for this recipe on page 52.

SALMON BLINTZES

1 7 3/4-oz. can salmon
1 c. cottage cheese
1 egg
2 tbsp. sugar
3/4 tsp. salt
1/4 tsp. cinnamon

12 Blintzes
Butter
1 c. sour cream
1/2 c. cherry or strawberry
  preserves

Drain and flake the salmon. Add the cottage cheese, egg, sugar, salt and cinnamon and mix thoroughly. Place about 2 tablespoons salmon mixture on the browned side of each Blintz and spread to within 1 inch of the edge. Fold bottom edge of the Blintz up about an inch over the filling. Fold the 2 sides of the Blintz in about 3/4 inch over the filling, then roll Blintz from the bottom. The Blintzes may be refrigerated until ready to use, if desired. Place Blintzes in a single layer in small amount of melted butter in a 10-inch frypan or chafing dish blazer pan. Cook over moderate heat for 5 to 6 minutes or until brown. Turn carefully and cook for 5 to 6 minutes longer or until brown. Drain on absorbent paper. Place 2 Blintzes on a small plate and top with sour cream and cherry preserves.

Blintzes

3/4 c. all-purpose flour
1/4 tsp. salt
1 c. milk

2 eggs, beaten
Oil

Combine the flour and salt in a bowl. Combine the milk and eggs and add to flour mixture gradually. Stir until smooth. Pour 2 tablespoons of batter into lightly oiled 6-inch frypan and tip the frypan so that the batter completely covers the bottom. Cook over moderate heat for 3 to 4 minutes or until brown on the bottom and set on top. Remove from frypan.

Salmon Blintzes (above)

Noodles Alfredo (page 74)

chafing dish vegetables, cereals and pastas

Party vegetables take on a special air when they are served from a chafing dish. *Southern Living* homemakers know this and make the most of their beautiful chafing dishes and delicious vegetable recipes. For your next party, try Gourmet Asparagus. This mouth-watering dish tastes extra-good when served from a chafing dish. And do try Chafing Dish Potato Pancakes. Chafing dishes seem to be made for pancakes — and when the pancakes are potato, your hungry guests will ask for more.

Cereals, too, seem to take on new elegance when served from chafing dishes. Nothing could be more typically southern than grits — and if you haven't yet discovered how good they can be, try preparing Cheese Grits for your next gathering. Another unusual recipe using cereal is Party Rice with Ham — two favorite southern foods combined into a dish sure to be a hit with any group!

In this section, you'll find pasta recipes developed just for chafing dish cooking. Macaroni . . . noodles . . . spaghetti . . . there are recipes galore! Pasta Jambalaya couldn't be more southern . . . or better tasting! And Oyster-Spaghetti Luisa is so easy to prepare . . . and so spectacular your guests will be talking about it for hours.

Yes, this is the section you'll want to read before your next party, for spectacular dishes that are delicious — and easy to prepare!

Mushrooms and Eggs in Cheese Sauce Supreme (below)

MUSHROOMS AND EGGS IN CHEESE SAUCE SUPREME

1 1/2 c. sliced mushrooms	Dash of pepper
1 tbsp. lemon juice	1 c. milk
1/4 c. butter	1 c. shredded Cheddar cheese
1/2 c. chopped celery	1/4 tsp. Worcestershire sauce
1/2 c. chopped green pepper	3 hard-cooked eggs
1/4 c. chopped onion	Rice
2 tbsp. all-purpose flour	Chow mein noodles
1/2 tsp. salt	

Toss the mushrooms with lemon juice. Melt the butter in a chafing dish blazer pan. Add the mushrooms, celery, green pepper and onion and saute until almost tender. Stir in the flour, salt and pepper and remove from heat. Stir in the milk gradually and cook over medium heat, stirring constantly, until thickened. Cook for 2 minutes longer and remove from heat. Add the cheese and Worcestershire sauce and stir until cheese is melted. Reserve 1 egg yolk and chop remaining eggs. Add to sauce and heat to serving temperature. Do not boil. Sieve remaining egg yolk and sprinkle on the mushroom mixture. Place blazer pan over burner. Serve mushroom mixture over rice and chow mein noodles. 6 servings.

GOURMET ASPARAGUS

2 tbsp. butter	1 can chicken and rice soup
2 tbsp. flour	1/2 c. milk

1/2 c. asparagus liquid
1/2 c. cooked onions, sieved
Dash of paprika

2 doz. stalks cooked
asparagus

Melt the butter in a blazer pan over hot water. Mix in the flour until well blended. Stir in the soup, milk and asparagus liquid and cook until thickened, stirring constantly. Stir in the onions, then sprinkle with paprika. Cook for several minutes, then add the asparagus. Heat through. 4-6 servings.

Mrs. Sam Cleveland, Fairmont, West Virginia

TURKISH BEANS

4 slices bacon, diced
1 med. onion, chopped
1 lge. tomato, chopped
2 No. 2 cans green beans,
   drained

1/2 tsp. sugar
1/2 tsp. salt
Dash of pepper
Dash of ground nutmeg

Brown the bacon in blazer dish pan over low heat, stirring constantly. Remove bacon from pan and reserve. Place the onion and tomato in the bacon fat and cook until onion is transparent. Add the beans, sugar, salt, pepper and nutmeg and heat through. Sprinkle with reserved bacon and place blazer pan over hot water. 8 servings.

Mrs. P. A. Hooper, Biloxi, Mississippi

MARINATED CHAFING DISH BEETS

1 can tiny whole beets,
   drained
1/2 c. vinegar
1/4 c. salad oil

1 tsp. salt
1/4 c. (firmly packed) brown
   sugar

Place the beets in a 1-quart jar. Mix remaining ingredients and pour over beets. Cover and shake well. Refrigerate for 2 days, shaking jar frequently. Place the beets and marinade in a chafing dish and heat through. Spear each beet with colored toothpick.

Mrs. Guy Smithson, Marble Falls, Texas

EGGPLANT CAPRI

3 tbsp. oil
1 eggplant, diced
1 sm. onion, diced
1 sm. green pepper, diced

1 clove of garlic, minced
1 No. 2 can tomatoes
1 bay leaf
Salt and pepper to taste

Heat the oil in blazer pan over low heat. Add the eggplant, onion, green pepper and garlic and cook until eggplant is brown. Add the tomatoes, bay leaf, salt and pepper and cover pan. Cook until eggplant is tender, then remove bay leaf. Place blazer pan over water pan and keep hot. 4 servings.

Mrs. David Langley, Decatur, Georgia

Peter Pancho Sauce with Cauliflower (below)

PETER PANCHO SAUCE WITH CAULIFLOWER

1 tbsp. butter	1/4 lb. American process
1 tbsp. flour	cheese, grated
1 1/2 c. milk	Hot crisp-cooked
1/2 c. smooth peanut butter	cauliflowerets

Melt the butter in a blazer pan over low heat and blend in flour. Stir in the milk gradually. Bring to a boil, stirring constantly, and boil for 1 minute. Add the peanut butter and cheese and stir until melted and well blended. Add the cauliflowerets and place blazer pan over hot water. Canned, drained sweet potatoes may be substituted for cauliflowerets.

SPICED CAULIFLOWER

1 med. cauliflower	1 tsp. tarragon vinegar
3 tbsp. butter	1/2 tsp. sweet marjoram
1 sm. onion, chopped	1/2 tsp. salt
2 anchovies, finely chopped	1/4 tsp. pepper

Cook the cauliflower in boiling water until tender. Drain and reserve 1 cup liquid. Separate the cauliflower into flowerets. Melt the butter in a blazer pan over low heat. Add the onion and anchovies and cook until onion is tender. Add reserved liquid, vinegar, marjoram, salt and pepper and bring to a boil. Add the cauliflower and heat through. Do not boil. Place blazer pan over water pan. Garnish cauliflower with slices of hard-cooked egg. 4-6 servings.

Laura Evelyn Lamar, Fort Smith, Arkansas

RATATOUILLE

1/3 c. olive oil	2 1/2 c. peeled diced eggplant
3/4 c. thinly sliced onions	3 c. zucchini, cut in 1/2-in. slices
2 cloves of garlic, minced	2 c. peeled quartered tomatoes
4 green peppers, cut in strips	Salt and pepper to taste

Combine all ingredients in a chafing dish and cover. Cook over low heat for 30 to 35 minutes. Uncover and cook for 10 minutes longer or until liquid has evaporated. Place over hot water. 8 servings.

Mrs. Ruth Henderson, Tulsa, Oklahoma

CHAFING DISH SUCCOTASH

1/2 c. light cream	1 1/2 c. cooked lima beans, drained
1 1/2 c. cooked whole	Salt and pepper to taste
kernel corn	2 tbsp. butter

Warm the cream in a blazer pan over hot water. Add the corn, lima beans, salt and pepper and heat through. Stir in the butter just before serving. 6 servings.

Mrs. E. H. Gilmer, Warrenton, North Carolina

CHAFING DISH POTATO PANCAKES

4 c. hot mashed potatoes	Salt and pepper to taste
2 eggs, beaten	Dash of ground nutmeg
3 tbsp. flour	4 tbsp. butter

Mix the potatoes with eggs, flour, salt, pepper and nutmeg, then beat until smooth. Cool. Shape into flat cakes, using 1 tablespoon for each, and refrigerate until chilled. Melt the butter in a chafing dish over medium flame. Add potato cakes and cook until done, turning once to brown both sides. Place blazer pan over hot water. 8 servings.

Mrs. Frances Oakley, Gadsden, Alabama

POTATO-ONION PANCAKES

2 lge. potatoes, grated	Pepper and nutmeg to taste
1 med. onion, grated	1/2 tsp. chopped parsley
2 tbsp. flour	2 eggs, separated
1/4 tsp. salt	Butter

Place the potatoes and onion in a bowl. Add the flour, salt, pepper, nutmeg and parsley and mix well. Add the beaten egg yolks and mix well. Fold in the stiffly beaten egg whites. Melt a small amount of butter in a chafing dish over medium-high flame. Add the potato mixture, 2 tablespoons at a time for each pancake, and fry until golden brown on both sides. Place blazer pan over hot water. 4-5 servings.

Mrs. Azalee S. Bowlin, Easley, South Carolina

CREAMED HASH POTATOES

1 clove of garlic, split	4 c. cubed cooked potatoes
2 tbsp. butter	Salt and pepper to taste
1/2 c. heavy cream	2 tbsp. chopped chives or
1/2 c. grated Swiss cheese	scallions

Rub garlic over blazer pan and place blazer pan over water pan. Melt butter in blazer pan. Add the cream and heat until warm. Add cheese and cover pan. Cook over low heat until cheese melts. Add the potatoes, salt and pepper and heat through. Sprinkle with chives. 6 servings.

Nina Putnam, Pensacola, Florida

CHAFING DISH POTATOES AU GRATIN

4 tbsp. butter	1/2 tsp. salt
3 tbsp. flour	1/4 tsp. pepper
2 c. milk	4 c. cubed cooked potatoes
1 c. grated American cheese	Chopped parsley to taste

Melt the butter in blazer pan over low heat, then blend in the flour. Add the milk gradually and cook, stirring constantly, for about 5 minutes, or until thickened. Add the cheese, salt and pepper and cook until cheese melts. Fold in potatoes gently and heat through. Sprinkle with parsley. Place blazer pan over water pan and keep hot. 6 servings.

Mrs. H. T. Smithson, Phoenix, Arizona

NARANJA SWEET POTATOES

3 tbsp. butter or margarine	1 med. orange, peeled
3 tbsp. orange juice	6 cooked yams, peeled and sliced
3 tbsp. brown sugar	2 tbsp. grated coconut (opt.)
1/2 tsp. grated lime or lemon rind	

Melt the butter in a blazer pan over hot water. Add the orange juice, sugar and grated rind and stir well. Cook for 5 minutes. Cut the orange in 6 slices and arrange the yams and orange slices in blazer pan. Cover and cook until the yams and orange slices are hot. Sprinkle with coconut. 6 servings.

Mrs. Frank Lowery, Grants, New Mexico

SWEET POTATOES ALEXANDRIA

4 tbsp. butter or margarine	6 ears of corn, cooked
6 cooked sweet potatoes,	1 green-tipped banana, cut in chunks
peeled and sliced	3 tbsp. corn syrup

Heat the butter in blazer pan over low heat. Add the potatoes and brown lightly on both sides. Cut the corn from the cob and add to potatoes. Arrange bananas on top. Pour in the corn syrup and cover. Cook until heated through. Place blazer pan over water pan and keep hot. 6 servings.

Lois McCarthy, Houston, Texas

GOLDEN GLORY BEETS WITH PINEAPPLE

1　13 1/2-oz. can pineapple chunks	2 1/2 tbsp. flour
1/2 c. water	1/2 tsp. seasoned salt
1/3 c. vinegar	2　1-lb. cans party-sliced beets, drained
3 tbsp. brown sugar	

Drain the pineapple and reserve syrup. Combine reserved syrup with water and vinegar in a blazer pan. Mix the brown sugar, flour and seasoned salt and stir into vinegar mixture. Cook and stir for about 10 minutes or until thickened. Add the beets and heat for several minutes longer. Add pineapple chunks and heat through. Place over water pan and keep hot. 6-8 servings.

Golden Glory Beets with Pineapple (above)

69

CHEESE GRITS

1 c. grits	1/8 tsp. garlic salt
1/2 c. butter	1/4 tsp. Worcestershire
1/2 lb. sharp cheese, grated	sauce
3 eggs, beaten	

Cook the grits according to package directions. Add the butter and cheese and stir until melted. Stir in remaining ingredients and place in blazer pan. Place blazer pan in water pan and cook until grits mixture is set. Serve with chicken or ham.

Mrs. M. L. Thompson, Dallas, Texas

GRITS AU GRATIN

4 c. cooked grits	Buttered bread crumbs,
1/3 lb. sharp cheese, grated	toasted
1/2 c. milk	Paprika

Place alternate layers of grits and cheese in a blazer pan. Pour milk over top and sprinkle with bread crumbs and paprika. Place over hot water and cook until milk is absorbed and cheese is melted. 6 servings.

Mrs. Frank Cress, Salisbury, North Carolina

TOMATO-GRITS AND CHEESE

1 8-oz. can tomato sauce	2 tsp. Worcestershire sauce
4 c. water	1 c. grits
1 tsp. salt	1 c. grated Cheddar cheese
1/4 tsp. pepper	

Mix the tomato sauce, water, salt, pepper and Worcestershire sauce in large blazer pan and bring to a boil. Stir in grits slowly and cover. Place blazer pan over water pan and cook until grits mixture is thick. Uncover and stir in the cheese. Cook until cheese is melted. 6 servings.

Mrs. W. C. Young, Paducah, Kentucky

RAJAHMUNDRY RICE

4 c. hot cooked rice	1/2 c. toasted slivered
1/2 tsp. curry powder	almonds
1/2 c. diced cooked celery	

Mix the rice, curry powder, celery and almonds and place in a blazer pan. Place in water pan and keep warm. Serve with pork, chicken or seafood.

Mrs. Leland Todd, Greenup, Kentucky

ALMOND RICE

3 c. hot cooked rice	1/2 c. toasted slivered
2 tbsp. margarine	almonds

Mix the rice, margarine and almonds in a blazer pan. Place the blazer pan over water pan and keep hot. Serve with poultry, seafood or beef.

Mrs. Hugh Griffin, Petersburg, Virginia

GREEN RICE

2 c. rice	2 green peppers, chopped
2 c. cream	2 sm. onions, chopped
2/3 c. cooking oil	1/2 c. chopped parsley
2 c. grated cheese	2 beaten eggs

Cook the rice according to package directions, then stir in remaining ingredients. Place in a blazer pan and place blazer pan in water pan. Cook for 45 minutes. 12 servings.

Mrs. Flora B. Mims, Memphis, Tennessee

PARTY RICE WITH HAM

3 tbsp. butter or margarine	2 8-oz. cans tomato sauce
1/4 c. minced green peppers	1 1/2 c. hot water or
1/4 c. minced onions	bouillon
1/4 c. sliced mushrooms	1 5-oz. package precooked
1/2 c. minced cooked ham	rice

Melt the butter in blazer pan over low heat. Add the green peppers, onions, mushrooms and ham and brown lightly. Pour in the tomato sauce and hot water and bring to a boil. Add the rice and cover pan. Cook until rice is done. Place blazer pan over water pan and keep hot. Fluff with a fork just before serving.

Mrs. J. L. Weldon, Newark, Delaware

SPANISH RICE PRONTO

1/4 c. bacon drippings or	2 8-oz. cans tomato sauce
butter	1 1/2 c. hot water
1 med. onion, thinly sliced	1 tsp. salt
1/2 med. green pepper, diced	Dash of pepper
1 1/3 c. instant rice	1/2 tsp. prepared mustard

Melt the bacon drippings in a blazer pan. Add the onion, green pepper and rice and cook over high heat, stirring, until brown. Add remaining ingredients and mix well. Bring to a boil and reduce heat. Simmer for 5 minutes. Place blazer pan over water pan and keep hot. 4 servings.

Brenda Warren, Andalusia, Alabama

EPICUREAN WILD RICE

1/3 c. butter or margarine	1 can consomme
1/2 c. snipped parsley	1 1/2 c. boiling water
1/2 c. chopped green onions	1 tsp. salt
1 c. diagonally sliced	1/2 tsp. dried marjoram
celery	1/2 c. sherry
1 1/4 c. wild rice	

Melt the butter in blazer of chafing dish. Add the parsley, onions and celery and saute until onions are soft but not browned. Add the rice, consomme, water, salt and marjoram and cover. Cook over direct heat for about 45 minutes or until rice is tender and liquid is absorbed, stirring occasionally and adding hot water, if needed. Remove cover and stir in the sherry. Cook for about 5 minutes longer or until sherry is absorbed, stirring occasionally. Place blazer pan over water pan and keep hot. 6 servings.

Mrs. Dan P. Johnston, Dallas, Texas

EXOTIC RICE CASSEROLE

2 c. rice	1 5-oz. can sliced water
2 cans beef consomme	chestnuts
2 lge. onions, chopped	1 4 1/2-oz. can mushroom
1 c. chopped celery	pieces
1 stick butter	

Cook rice according to package directions, substituting consomme for water. Saute the onions and celery in butter in a blazer pan until soft and light brown. Add water chestnuts and mushrooms and simmer for 10 to 15 minutes. Add the rice. Cover and cook for 15 minutes longer. Place the blazer pan over water pan and keep hot. 10-12 servings.

Mrs. Mayme McLean, Liberty, Texas

PASTA JAMBALAYA

3 tbsp. butter or margarine	1 tsp. salt
1 green pepper, finely diced	1/4 tsp. pepper
2 lge. onions, finely diced	1 1/2 c. diced cooked
1 clove of garlic	chicken
3 1/2 c. cooked tomatoes	5 c. cooked macaroni
1 tbsp. chili powder	1 tbsp. vinegar

Heat the butter in blazer pan over low heat. Add the green pepper, onions and garlic and cook until onions are transparent. Discard garlic. Pour in tomatoes, chili powder, salt and pepper and cover. Cook for about 20 minutes, stirring occasionally. Add the chicken, macaroni and vinegar and mix well. Cook until heated through. Place over water and keep hot. Veal or lamb may be substituted for chicken. 6-8 servings.

Mrs. V. E. Linden, Huntington, West Virginia

MILANO MACARONI

2 tbsp. butter or margarine
1 med. onion, grated
1 c. milk
1 c. grated American cheese

1 tsp. prepared mustard
1/4 c. shredded pimento
6 c. cooked macaroni

Melt the butter in blazer pan over low heat. Add the onion and cook until soft. Place blazer pan over hot water. Stir in the milk, cheese, mustard, and pimento and cook over low heat, stirring frequently, until cheese is melted. Stir in the macaroni and heat through. 8 servings.

Nancy Summerfield, Johnson City, Tennessee

NOODLE PARTY PANCAKES

4 c. fine egg noodles
2 eggs

3/4 tsp. salt
Melted butter or margarine

Cook the noodles in boiling, salted water until tender and drain. Beat the eggs with salt in a large bowl and stir in 1/4 cup melted butter. Add the noodles and toss until mixed. Pour about 3 tablespoons butter into a skillet or chafing dish blazer pan over medium heat. Drop noodle mixture by tablespoonfuls into butter and cook on both sides until golden brown, adding butter as needed. Serve hot with sour cream and caviar. 4-6 servings.

Noodle Party Pancakes (above)

73

NOODLES ALFREDO

1/4 c. salt	1 lb. butter, softened
8 to 12 qt. boiling water	4 c. grated Parmesan cheese
2 lb. medium egg noodles	1 c. heavy cream

Add the salt to boiling water in a large saucepan and add the noodles gradually so water continues to boil. Cook, stirring occasionally, until tender and drain in a colander. Place the butter in a hot chafing dish. Add the noodles and toss gently. Add the cheese and toss. Pour in the cream and toss. Sprinkle with pepper, if desired. 12-16 servings.

Photograph for this recipe on page 62.

NOODLES VALIENTI

1/2 lb. egg noodles	1 sm. clove of garlic, minced
1/4 c. butter or margarine	1 c. creamed cottage cheese
2 tbsp. finely chopped onion	1 c. sour cream
	1/2 tsp. salt

Cook the noodles according to package directions and drain. Melt the butter in blazer pan of chafing dish over high heat. Add the onion and garlic and cook until tender, stirring constantly. Reduce heat. Stir in the cheese, sour cream and salt and mix. Add the noodles and toss to coat well. Heat through and garnish with parsley. Place blazer pan over water pan and keep warm. 4 servings.

Mrs. Betty Everette, New Orleans, Louisiana

FETTUCINE IN TUNA SAUCE

1 1/2 c. fettucine or noodles	2 tbsp. butter
1 4-oz. can sliced mushrooms	2 tbsp. flour
1 7-oz. can tuna	1/2 tsp. salt
1 c. evaporated milk	1/8 tsp. white pepper
	1 c. garlic croutons

Cook the fettucine according to package directions and drain. Drain the mushrooms and tuna and reserve liquids. Mix reserved liquids with milk and add enough water to make 2 cups liquid. Melt the butter in blazer pan and blend in flour, salt and pepper. Stir in the milk mixture gradually. Place over hot water and cook, stirring constantly, until thickened. Add the tuna, mushrooms and fettucine and heat through. Sprinkle with croutons and serve hot. 4-6 servings.

Mrs. A. C. Norris, Tifton, Georgia

BUTTERED PARMESAN NOODLES

1 1-lb. package egg noodles	1/4 lb. butter
1 egg yolk, beaten	1/2 c. grated Parmesan cheese
1/3 c. light cream	

Cook the noodles according to package directions and drain. Keep warm. Mix the egg yolk with cream. Melt the butter in blazer pan over hot water and stir in the noodles. Add the cream mixture and cheese and toss well. 4-6 servings.

Mrs. Paul Graham, Fort Smith, Arkansas

OYSTER-SPAGHETTI LUISA

1 1/2 c. spaghetti	1 tbsp. flour
1 4-oz. can sliced	1 tsp. salt
mushrooms	1/8 tsp. pepper
Chicken broth	1 pt. oysters, drained
1 c. light cream	1/4 c. grated Parmesan
3 tbsp. butter	cheese

Cook the spaghetti according to package directions and drain. Drain the mushrooms and reserve liquid. Add enough chicken broth to reserved mushroom liquid to make 1/2 cup liquid. Add the cream. Melt the butter in blazer pan over low heat and stir in the flour, salt, and pepper until smooth. Add the broth mixture slowly and cook, stirring constantly, until mixture comes almost to a boil. Add oysters and mushrooms and cook until edges of oysters curl. Stir in spaghetti. Sprinkle with cheese and dot with additional butter. Place blazer pan over water pan and keep hot. 4 servings.

Mrs. Catherine Williams, Tuscumbia, Alabama

SPAGHETTI WITH FRANKFURTERS

1 15 1/4-oz. can spaghetti	1/4 c. chopped green
in tomato sauce with cheese	pepper (opt.)
1/2 lb. frankfurters, sliced	1/2 c. shredded Cheddar
1 2-oz. can sliced	cheese
mushrooms, drained	1/2 tsp. oregano (opt.)

Combine all ingredients in blazer pan of chafing dish and mix. Cover and heat to serving temperature over moderate heat, stirring frequently. Place over water pan and keep hot. 3-4 servings.

Mrs. Jean Flowers, St. Petersburg, Florida

SPAGHETTI WITH CHICKEN LIVERS

1 12-oz. package spaghetti	1 c. sliced mushrooms
1/4 c. butter	Salt and pepper to taste
1 tsp. vinegar	2 c. tomato sauce
2 c. chicken livers, cut in halves	

Cook the spaghetti according to package directions and drain. Melt the butter in blazer pan and add vinegar, chicken livers and mushrooms. Cook for 5 to 10 minutes or until chicken livers are light brown. Season with salt and pepper. Stir in the tomato sauce and heat through. Add the spaghetti and stir well. Place over hot water and keep hot. 6 servings.

Mrs. M. F. James, Palm Beach, Florida

(Clockwise) Fresh Corn Chowder (page 86);
Fresh Corn-Seafood Chowder (page 86);
Fresh Corn-Cheese Soup (page 84)

chafing dish soups and chowders

Few party dishes are more eye-appealing than a beautiful silver or copper chafing dish filled with shimmering soup or chowder. Southern homemakers know that soups taste delicious . . . smell heavenly . . . and are the perfect food for many different types of gatherings. And they have developed many prized recipes which they share with you in the pages that follow.

You know how easy it is to sparkle up a family supper by serving soup or chowder from the chafing dish — the soup is no different from usual, but somehow it tastes different! With this collection of great soup and chowder recipes, you can bring your family and guests an endless variety of soup and chowder treats.

One southern favorite is Chicken and Oyster Gumbo — a rich, thick, uniquely southern soup that is almost a meal in itself. Another is Chafing Dish Chili — hot, hearty, and utterly delicious. Springtime Shrimp Bisque . . . Borsch with Sour Cream . . . Green Pea Soup With Mushrooms . . . these are just a few of the soups southern women serve their delighted families and guests.

Every one of these recipes — and many more — are in the following section. Some of them can be prepared right in your very best chafing dish while others are prepared in the kitchen — simmering for long, slow hours on the back of the stove — and served from a chafing dish. All are certain to bring you warm compliments.

Mediterranean Sandwich Soup (below)

MEDITERRANEAN SANDWICH SOUP

1 2/3 c. canned pitted ripe
   olives
1 lge. green pepper
1 lge. tomato
1 lge. onion
2 cloves of garlic, crushed
1 tsp. salt
2 c. grated Cheddar cheese

1 c. chicken stock or onion
   soup
6 thick slices French bread
Olive oil
6 slices chicken
6 slices ham
1/2 c. grated Parmesan
   cheese

Cut the ripe olives in quarters. Cut the green pepper and tomato in half, scoop out membrane, seeds and juice and dice. Dice the onion and mix with green pepper, tomato, garlic, ripe olives, salt, cheese and stock. Place in chafing dish blazer pan and heat over low heat, stirring, until cheese is melted. Place over hot water. Brush both sides of bread with oil and place on a cookie sheet. Bake at 350 degrees for 25 minutes or until brown, turning once. Arrange bread slices on a serving platter and place chicken and ham on bread. Top with ripe olive mixture and Parmesan cheese. 6 servings.

AVGOLEMONO SOUP

6 c. chicken broth
1/3 c. rice

3 eggs
1/3 c. lemon juice

Bring chicken broth to a boil in a deep blazer pan and add rice. Simmer for about 20 minutes or until rice is tender. Beat the eggs well and stir in the lemon juice. Add 2 cups hot broth slowly, stirring constantly. Stir back into remaining broth and cook, stirring constantly, until heated through. Do not boil. Place over water pan and keep hot. 4-6 servings.

Mrs. Wilma Dunias, Lubbock, Texas

CHICKEN AND OYSTER GUMBO

1 3 to 5-lb. chicken	1/2 c. green onion tops
1/3 c. shortening	1/4 c. chopped parsley
1/2 c. flour	1 pt. oysters
1 lge. onion, chopped	1 tbsp. file
Salt and pepper to taste	

Cut the chicken in serving pieces and brown in shortening in a skillet. Place in a kettle and add 2 quarts boiling water. Bring to a boil, then simmer. Add the flour to shortening in the skillet and cook over low heat, stirring, until light brown. Add the onion and cook until brown, stirring constantly. Stir in 2 cups chicken stock from kettle until smooth, then stir back into stock in kettle. Cook until chicken is tender, stirring frequently. Add remaining ingredients and cook for 10 minutes longer. Place in a deep blazer pan and place blazer pan over hot water.

Mrs. Lee Holder, Atmore, Alabama

FLEMISH BEEF SOUP

1/4 c. flour	1 bay leaf
2 tsp. salt	1/2 tsp. crumbled thyme
1/4 tsp. pepper	2 tbsp. vinegar
2 lb. lean stew beef	1 pkg. frozen stew
2 tbsp. cooking oil	vegetables
1 med. onion, chopped	1 sm. package frozen peas
1 tbsp. brown sugar	2 tbsp. chopped
1 12-oz. can beer	parsley (opt.)
1 10 1/2-oz. can beef broth	

Mix the flour, salt and pepper. Cut the stew beef in 1 1/2-inch cubes and mix with flour mixture. Heat the oil in a kettle and add the beef. Brown over medium heat on all sides. Add the onion and cook for 3 to 4 minutes or until onion is soft. Add the brown sugar, beer, beef broth, bay leaf, thyme and vinegar and bring to boiling point. Cover. Simmer for about 1 hour or until beef is tender. Bring to boiling point and add frozen vegetables. Sprinkle with additional salt and pepper to taste. Place in a blazer pan and place over water pan. Cover and cook for 20 minutes. Add the peas and cook for 15 minutes longer. Remove bay leaf and sprinkle with chopped parsley. 6 servings.

Mrs. Donald E. Harms, Ft. Wright, Kentucky

CHAFING DISH CHILI

1 lge. onion, chopped
1 green pepper, chopped
2 tbsp. olive oil
1 1/2 lb. ground beef,
    crumbled
1 can tomato soup

1 tbsp. chili powder
1 1/2 tsp. salt
Dash of cayenne pepper
1/4 c. chopped parsley
1 can kidney beans, drained

Saute the onion and green pepper in oil in a large blazer pan until tender. Add ground beef and cook until brown, stirring frequently. Add remaining ingredients except beans and simmer for 15 minutes. Add the beans and cook for 15 minutes longer. Place over water pan and keep hot.

Alma E. Shepherd, Alexandria, Virginia

CHAFING DISH GOULASH WITH NOODLES

1/3 c. butter or margarine
3 med. onions, sliced
2 med. green peppers, chopped
1 1/2 tbsp. salt
3 to 4 tsp. paprika

2 1/2 lb. boned beef rump
2 1-lb. cans tomatoes,
    drained
2 8-oz. cans tomato sauce

Melt the butter in a skillet. Add onions and green peppers and saute for 5 minutes, stirring frequently. Add the salt and paprika. Cut the beef in 1-inch cubes and add to onion mixture. Add 3 1/2 cups water and tomatoes. Cook, covered, for 1 hour or until beef is almost tender. Add the tomato sauce and place in a blazer pan over hot water. Cook for 10 minutes, stirring occasionally. Serve with parslied noodles.

Mrs. S. T. Weldon, Houston, Texas

MEXICAN SOUP DE ALBONDIGAS

1 tbsp. bacon fat
1/2 c. chopped onion
2 No. 2 cans hominy, well
    drained
2 c. cooked tomatoes
3 c. chicken stock
1/2 lb. hamburger
1/4 c. cornmeal

1/4 clove of garlic, minced
1/2 c. grated onion
1/2 tsp. salt
1/4 tsp. pepper
1/4 tsp. monosodium glutamate
1 beaten egg
1/2 tsp. chili powder (opt.)

Melt bacon fat in large chafing dish. Add the onion and saute until tender. Add the hominy, tomatoes and chicken stock and bring to a boil. Mix the hamburger, cornmeal, garlic, onion, salt, pepper, monosodium glutamate and egg and form into tiny balls. Drop into boiling soup mixture and simmer for 1 hour. Place over hot water and stir in the chili powder. Keep hot. 8 servings.

Mrs. Perry J. Adams, Fort Worth, Texas

OXTAIL SOUP

1 1/2 lb. oxtail	1/2 c. diced onion
1 1/2 qt. boiling water	1/2 c. diced celery
1 tbsp. salt	3/4 c. diced carrots
2 tbsp. rice	1 c. cooked tomatoes

Cut the oxtail in 2-inch pieces and brown in small amount of hot fat in a kettle. Add the water and salt and simmer, covered, for about 2 hours or until meat is tender. Remove oxtail from broth and cool. Remove meat from bones and add to broth. Pour into large chafing dish. Add the rice, onion, celery and carrots and cover. Simmer for 30 minutes. Skim off most of the fat and add tomatoes. Simmer until tomatoes are heated. Place over hot water.

Mabel B. Couch, Chelsea, Oklahoma

TOMATO MOUSERON

2 lb. boneless stew beef	1 lge. green pepper, chopped
1/4 lb. shortening	4 ripe tomatoes, chopped
2 med. onions, chopped	1 sm. can mushrooms
1 c. chopped celery	Salt and pepper to taste

Cut the beef in small pieces and brown in shortening in a skillet. Add 4 cups water, onions, celery, green pepper and tomatoes and simmer for 1 hour or until beef is tender. Add the mushrooms, salt and pepper and place in blazer pan over hot water. Cook for about 20 minutes. One large can tomatoes may be substituted for fresh tomatoes. 6-8 servings.

Janet Sorenson, Rockport, Texas

GREEN BEANS FAGIDINI

2 lb. beef stew meat or pork shoulder	1/2 tsp. pepper
2 tbsp. oil	2 tbsp. chopped parsley
1 lge. onion, finely chopped	2 c. tomatoes
1 tsp. salt	2 c. water
	4 c. fresh beans, snapped

Cut the meat in small pieces and brown in oil in a skillet. Add the onion, salt, pepper and parsley and cook until onion is tender. Add tomatoes and water. Cook over low heat for about 1 hour. Add the beans and place in blazer pan. Cook until beans are tender. Place over hot water. 8 servings.

Mrs. Max Phelps, Midland, Texas

CREOLE GUMBO

1 to 2 lb. fresh okra, sliced
6 green onions, chopped
1 lge. green pepper, chopped
5 celery stalks with leaves,
   chopped
1 stick margarine
1 8-oz. can tomato sauce
2 cans beef bouillon

2 bouillon cans water
1 6-oz. can crab meat
1 6-oz. can shrimp
2 tbsp. file (opt.)
1 tbsp. salt
1 tbsp. sugar
2 tbsp. vinegar

Cook the okra, onions, green pepper and celery in chafing dish in melted margarine until onions are golden brown, stirring constantly. Add the tomato sauce, beef bouillon, water, crab meat, shrimp and seasonings. Simmer for 1 hour. Place over hot water and serve over rice. 4-6 servings.

Mrs. Robert Overing, Chapin, South Carolina

TOMATO-CLAM SOUP

2 cans tomato soup
1 c. clam juice
1 soup can water

1/4 tsp. leaf thyme,
   crushed
1 can minced clams

Combine all ingredients in a blazer pan and place over water pan. Heat through, stirring occasionally. 4-6 servings.

Tomato-Clam Soup (above)

SALMON SOUP

1 can salmon	1/4 c. butter
1 qt. milk	Salt and pepper to taste

Remove bones from salmon. Place salmon in a blazer pan and mash. Stir in the milk, butter, salt and pepper and place over hot water. Heat to serving temperature.

Stella Vaughn, South Coffeyville, Oklahoma

SPRINGTIME SHRIMP BISQUE

2 cans cream of mushroom soup	1 c. cooked cleaned shrimp
1 tbsp. instant minced onion	2 tbsp. diced pimento
2 c. milk	1/8 tsp. salt
1 tbsp. butter or margarine	1 lge. avocado

Combine the soup and onion in chafing dish. Add milk gradually and stir until smooth. Place over hot water and heat through. Add the butter, shrimp, pimento and salt. Cut avocado in half and remove seed and skin. Dice avocado and place in soup. Cook until avocado is heated through. 5 servings.

Mrs. A. G. Jewett, Jr., Beaumont, Texas

CREAMY ASPARAGUS SOUP

1 10-oz. package frozen cut asparagus	Salt to taste
2 tbsp. butter or margarine	2 or 3 drops of hot sauce (opt.)
2 tsp. all-purpose flour	Dash of pepper
2 c. milk, scalded	1 c. grated American process cheese

Cook the asparagus according to package directions and drain. Melt the butter over low heat in blazer pan. Blend in the flour. Add the milk and cook, stirring constantly, until thickened. Add the asparagus, salt, hot sauce, and pepper and mix well. Add the cheese and heat, stirring constantly, until melted. Place blazer pan over hot water. 4-6 servings.

Mrs. Rhonda Cooper, Lawton, Oklahoma

CHAFING DISH BEAN SOUP

2 cans bean soup	1 hard-boiled egg, sieved
1/4 c. sherry	

Combine the bean soup with 2 soup cans water in a blazer pan. Place over low heat and bring to boiling point. Add the sherry and cook for 5 minutes. Place over hot water. Garnish soup with sieved egg.

Betty Evans, Durham, North Carolina

PASTA FAGIOLI

1/4 c. chopped celery	1 can tomato soup
1/4 c. chopped onion	1 soup can water
1 tbsp. chopped parsley	1 1-lb. 4-oz. can kidney
1 tsp. crushed oregano	beans, drained
1 sm. clove of garlic,	1/2 c. cooked elbow macaroni
minced	1/2 tsp. lemon juice
1 tbsp. olive oil	

Cook the celery, onion, parsley, oregano and garlic in oil in blazer pan until vegetables are tender. Add remaining ingredients and place blazer pan over water pan. Cook, stirring occasionally, until heated through. 3-4 servings.

Mrs. Anona Moore, Alvin, Texas

FRESH CORN-CHEESE SOUP

1 c. chopped onion	4 c. fresh corn, cut from cob
1 clove of garlic, chopped	4 c. milk
1 c. diced celery	1/4 tsp. chili powder
1/4 c. butter or margarine	1/4 tsp. pepper
1/4 c. flour	1/16 tsp. cayenne pepper
1 1/2 tsp. salt	2 c. shredded American
2 c. hot water	cheese
1/2 c. diced carrots	2 tbsp. lemon juice

Saute the onion, garlic and celery in butter in a blazer pan for about 10 minutes or until limp. Blend in the flour and salt. Remove from heat and add water. Cook, stirring, until smooth and medium thick. Add the carrots and corn and simmer for 15 minutes. Add the milk, seasonings and cheese and heat for 5 minutes or just until cheese melts. Do not boil. Place over water pan and keep hot. Stir in lemon juice before serving. Add hot water if soup thickens. Garnish with cooked and quartered ears of fresh corn, if desired. 2 quarts.

Photograph for this recipe on page 76.

MAIZE SOUP

1/2 c. finely chopped onion	Dash of pepper
1/4 c. grated carrot	2 chicken bouillon cubes,
2 tbsp. finely chopped	crushed
green pepper	2 c. milk, scalded
3 tbsp. butter or margarine	1 17-oz. can cream-style
2 tbsp. flour	corn

Cook the onion, carrot and green pepper in butter in blazer pan over low heat until tender. Blend in flour and pepper. Add bouillon, milk and corn and cook, stirring occasionally, until heated through. Place over hot water. 6-8 servings.

Mrs. T. W. Hitchcock, Rock Hill, South Carolina

BORSCH WITH SOUR CREAM

2 tbsp. shortening	1 c. canned tomatoes, sieved
1 med. onion, chopped	3/4 c. beet juice
3/4 c. diced potatoes	1 c. diced cooked beets
3/4 c. diced carrots	1 tbsp. lemon juice
3/4 c. shredded cabbage	1 tsp. salt
3/4 c. chopped celery	1/8 tsp. pepper
2 qt. beef stock	3/4 c. sour cream

Melt the shortening in a chafing dish. Add the onion and saute until golden. Add the potatoes, carrots, cabbage, celery and beef stock and simmer for 30 minutes. Add tomatoes, beet juice, beets, lemon juice, salt and pepper and cook until heated through. Place over hot water. Garnish each serving with 1 tablespoon sour cream. 8-10 servings.

Mrs. Emma S. Thomas, Alexander City, Alabama

ONION-CHICKEN SOUP AU VIN

2 c. sliced yellow onions	8 French bread slices,
1/4 c. butter or margarine	toasted
2 cans chicken broth	Grated Parmesan cheese
1/2 c. dry white wine	

Cook the onions in butter in blazer pan over low heat until browned. Add the broth, 1 1/3 cups water and wine and heat through. Place blazer pan over hot water. Serve soup in bowls. Sprinkle toast slices with cheese and float on soup. 8 servings.

Mrs. Raymond Patrick, Oakland, Maryland

GREEN PEA SOUP WITH MUSHROOMS

1 can green pea soup	3/4 c. diced cooked carrots
1 soup can milk	1 tsp. grated onion
1 4-oz. can mushroom pieces	

Mix the soup and milk in a blazer pan. Add remaining ingredients and mix well. Place over water pan and cook until heated through. 3-4 servings.

Mrs. Kenneth Hood, Dover, Delaware

PEA SOUP SUPREME

2 doz. small cooked onions	1 c. light cream
1 No. 2 can peas and liquid	2 tbsp. butter or margarine
1 can cream of mushroom soup	Salt and pepper to taste

Combine all ingredients in blazer pan placed over hot water and cover. Cook over low heat, stirring occasionally, until heated through. 4 servings.

Mrs. Roy Bolton, Louisville, Kentucky

Mushroom-Cheese Casserole (page 188), Fresh Corn Chowder (below)

FRESH CORN CHOWDER

4 ears of corn	1/8 tsp. pepper
3 c. milk	6 pats butter or margarine
2 tsp. salt	Chopped parsley

Husk corn and remove silks. Split each row of kernels lengthwise with a sharp knife and cut a thin layer of corn from the cob. Repeat, cutting 2 more layers. Scrape cob with the bowl of a tablespoon to extract all the liquid. The tablespoon prevents corn from spattering. Cook corn and milk in the top of a double boiler or chafing dish blazer pan over low heat for 30 minutes or until corn is slightly thickened and hot. Stir in the salt and pepper and place over hot water. Serve in soup bowls with a pat of butter on each serving. Sprinkle with parsley. 6 servings.

Photographs for this recipe above and on page 76.

FRESH CORN-SEAFOOD CHOWDER

2 1/2 c. water	2 tbsp. butter or margarine
1 1/2 tsp. salt	1 1/2 c. diced potatoes
6 peppercorns	1/2 12-oz. package frozen
3 whole cloves	fish fillets
1 sm. bay leaf	2 c. fresh corn, cut from cob
4 frozen lobster-tails	1 c. light cream or
6 chowder clams	evaporated milk
1/2 c. chopped onion	1/4 tsp. ground thyme
1 clove of garlic, chopped	

Place the water, salt, peppercorns, cloves and bay leaf in a large saucepan and bring to boiling point. Add lobster-tails and clams and cover. Cook for 12 to 15 minutes or until lobster turns pink and clam shells open. Drain and reserve liquid. Remove lobster and clams from shells and set aside. Saute the onion and garlic in butter in a blazer pan until limp and transparent. Strain reserved stock and stir into onion mixture. Add potatoes and fish and cover. Cook over low heat for 15 minutes or until potatoes are tender and fish is flaky. Add the corn, cream and thyme and cover. Cook over low heat for 10 minutes. Do not boil. Place over hot water. 1 1/2 quarts.

Photograph for this recipe on page 76.

CORN AND DRIED BEEF CHOWDER

1/2 c. chopped onion	1 c. milk
1 pkg. dried beef, chopped	2 tbsp. flour
2 tbsp. butter	1 can corn
1 c. water	Salt and pepper to taste
2 c. finely diced potatoes	

Saute the onion and dried beef in chafing dish in butter until onion is tender. Add the water and potatoes and cover. Simmer until potatoes are tender. Blend milk and flour and stir into potato mixture. Add corn and bring to a boil. Season with salt and pepper and place over water pan. Keep hot.

Mrs. Irma Dunn, Kingsport, Tennessee

ROAN CHOWDER

1/2 lb. ground round steak	1 sm. can tiny peas and
1/2 lb. bulk pork sausage	liquid
1 onion, chopped	1 1/2 c. noodles
1 lge. can tomatoes and	1 sm. can ripe olives, pitted
liquid	1/2 lb. grated cheese

Brown the meats and onion in a kettle. Add the tomatoes, peas, noodles and olives and cover. Cook over low heat for 1 hour. Place in blazer pan and place blazer pan over hot water. Add the cheese and stir until melted.

Mrs. Warren Fluker, Mobile, Alabama

CLAM CHOWDER

1/4 c. butter	1 c. water
2 sm. potatoes, diced	1 8-oz. can minced clams
1 med. onion, diced	Salt and pepper to taste
1/2 green pepper, diced	2 c. milk

Melt the butter in a chafing dish. Add the potatoes, onion and green pepper and cook until onion is tender. Add the water, clams and seasonings and cook over low heat until vegetables are done. Add milk and heat through. Place over hot water. May be thickened, if desired. 3-4 servings.

Kathryn Morgan, Memphis, Tennessee

Peppered Eggs and Salmon (page 93)

chafing dish eggs

Chafing dishes seem made just for eggs! Even the traditional Sunday morning scrambled eggs taste like a party treat when Mom prepares them in the chafing dish. Southern women know that many different kinds of egg dishes can be prepared in a chafing dish — and it makes sense to them to cook these dishes because of the low cost of eggs.

Because eggs are so popular, so nutritious, and such a good bargain, *Southern Living* homemakers have turned their imaginative talents toward creating a wide range of chafing dish egg recipes. The very best of these recipes are now yours, in the pages that follow. All the recipes in this section have been painstakingly developed . . . carefully perfected . . . and served with pride to family and friends.

You'll discover a recipe for a mouth-watering French Omelet . . . tangy Eggs Gruyere . . . and sharply flavored Eggs Louisianne. From the famous Alabama resort town comes a recipe for Eggs Point Clear. All of these recipes have brought praise to the women who developed them. Now they are yours to try, in this section.

Why not experiment with these easy-to-prepare recipes and create your own versions — perhaps an omelet that is uniquely yours or Herbed Scrambled Eggs featuring your family's favorite herb blend or a brand-new way to prepare poached eggs. Served in a chafing dish, your egg recipes are certain to taste extra-good!

FRENCH OMELET

4 eggs	Salt and pepper to taste
2 tbsp. water	1 tbsp. butter

Beat the eggs with the water in a bowl and add salt and pepper. Melt the butter in a blazer pan. Pour in the egg mixture and cook over low heat until set around the edges. Pull the omelet away from the edges of the pan with a fork, rolling the pan to allow the uncooked egg to seep down underneath. Cook until eggs are set but not dry. Fold the omelet and place the blazer pan over water pan. Keep warm. 2 servings.

Mrs. Cleda Freeman, Trinidad, Texas

EGGS LE GRANDE

2 tbsp. butter	1/4 tsp. pepper
1 tbsp. flour	1/2 c. cottage cheese
1 c. milk	5 hard-cooked eggs, quartered
1/2 tsp. salt	3 tbsp. chopped chives

Melt the butter in blazer pan over low heat. Add the flour and mix well. Stir in the milk, salt and pepper and cook for about 10 minutes, stirring constantly. Cream the cottage cheese in a bowl until smooth, then blend into the sauce. Spoon eggs into sauce and place the pan over hot water. Cook until eggs are hot. Sprinkle with chives and keep warm. 4 servings.

Mrs. Myron Cagle, Greensboro, North Carolina

EGGS JOYALE

3 tbsp. butter or margarine	3 tbsp. grated Parmesan
1/4 c. minced onions	cheese
4 eggs	

Melt the butter in a blazer pan over low heat. Add the onions and cook until tender but not brown. Place blazer pan over hot water. Place the eggs in the pan, one at a time, and keep separated. Sprinkle with cheese and cover the pan. Cook eggs to desired doneness. Serve with buttered toast.

Mrs. Anne Mims, Headland, Alabama

EGGS POINT CLEAR

5 eggs, beaten	2 c. crab meat, flaked
1/4 c. milk	2 tbsp. butter
Salt and pepper to taste	

Mix the eggs, milk, seasonings and crab meat. Melt the butter in blazer pan over hot water. Add crab meat mixture and cook until eggs are set, stirring constantly. 4-6 servings.

Holley Thorpe, Shawnee, Oklahoma

BAKED OMELET WITH CHEESE SAUCE

6 eggs, separated	1 tbsp. margarine
1 1/4 tsp. salt	1 c. milk
5 tbsp. cornstarch	2 c. shredded Cheddar cheese
Pepper	1/4 c. chopped pimento
1/3 c. water	

Preheat oven to 350 degrees. Place 2 greased 9-inch pie plates in oven and heat for about 5 minutes. Place the egg whites and 1 teaspoon salt in a bowl and beat with electric mixer until soft peaks form. Beat egg yolks until thick and lemon-colored, then beat in 4 tablespoons cornstarch and dash of pepper. Add the water and beat well. Fold egg yolk mixture into beaten egg whites and pour into the heated pie plates. Bake for about 15 minutes or until set. Melt the margarine in a small chafing dish blazer pan and remove from heat. Blend in remaining cornstarch, then stir in milk gradually. Add remaining salt and dash of pepper and bring to a boil over medium heat, stirring constantly. Boil for 1 minute. Add the cheese and stir just until melted. Stir in pimento. Set over hot water pan to keep hot. Turn 1 omelet out of pie plate onto serving platter and cover with half the sauce. Place remaining omelet on top and serve with remaining sauce. 4-6 servings.

Baked Omelet with Cheese Sauce (above)

EGGS GRUYERE

4 tbsp. butter	1/2 tsp. salt
1/2 c. cream	1/4 tsp. dried dill
1/2 lb. Gruyere cheese,	3 tbsp. sherry
grated	Toast rounds, spread with
6 eggs, beaten slightly	Smithfield ham spread

Melt 2 tablespoons butter in a blazer pan over low heat and stir in the cream. Place over water pan. Add the cheese and cook, stirring, until melted. Add the eggs and salt and cook, stirring constantly, until eggs are softly scrambled. Dot with remaining butter and sprinkle with dill and sherry. Serve on toast rounds. 4 servings.

Mrs. Margie Jones, Waco, Texas

EGGS LOUISIANNE

3 tbsp. olive oil	1/2 tsp. chili powder
1 med. onion, chopped fine	1/2 tsp. salt
1 pimento, chopped fine	1/4 tsp. pepper
1 green pepper, chopped fine	2 chicken bouillon cubes
6 eggs, beaten lightly	1 1/2 c. hot water

Heat the oil in a blazer pan over low heat. Add the onion, pimento and green pepper and cook until onion is golden. Add the eggs and seasonings and cook for several minutes, stirring occasionally. Dissolve bouillon cubes in hot water, then pour over egg mixture. Cover and cook for several minutes longer. Place blazer pan over water pan and keep warm. 4 servings.

Mrs. Rozanna Plante, Tuscaloosa, Alabama

DELICIOUS ALMOND EGGS

3 tbsp. butter	1/8 tsp. pepper
3/4 c. sliced mushrooms	1/2 c. light cream
6 eggs, slightly beaten	1/2 c. blanched slivered
1 tsp. salt	almonds

Melt the butter in blazer pan over low heat. Add the mushrooms and cook until soft. Place pan over hot water. Add the eggs, salt, pepper and cream and cook to desired doneness, stirring constantly. Sprinkle with almonds and keep warm. 4 servings.

Mrs. Paul Smith, Prattville, Alabama

HERBED SCRAMBLED EGGS

8 eggs	1 tsp. chopped parsley
1 tsp. salt	1 tsp. chopped chives
1/4 tsp. pepper	3 tbsp. butter

Combine all ingredients except butter in a bowl and beat until well blended. Heat the butter in blazer pan over hot water. Pour in the egg mixture and cook over low heat, stirring constantly, until eggs are done. Cover and keep warm. 4 servings.

Mrs. M. Hamilton, Greensboro, North Carolina

PEPPERED EGGS AND SALMON

1 1-lb. can salmon, drained	1 green pepper, diced
3 strips bacon	1/2 tsp. salt
2 tbsp. butter	1/4 tsp. cayenne pepper
1/2 c. chopped green onions with tops	6 eggs, lightly beaten
	1/4 c. light cream
	1 tsp. Worcestershire sauce

Flake the salmon and set aside. Saute the bacon in chafing dish blazer pan until crisp and drain on absorbent paper. Crumble the bacon. Pour off bacon fat from blazer pan and melt the butter in same blazer pan. Saute the onions and green pepper in butter for about 5 minutes or until onions are transparent. Add the seasonings and salmon. Mix the eggs, cream and Worcestershire sauce. Add to onion mixture and cook over moderate heat, stirring constantly, until eggs are set. Place over warm water and sprinkle with bacon. 4 servings.

Photograph for this recipe on page 88.

HOT HOLIDAY DEVILED EGGS

20 hard-cooked eggs	1 1/2 tbsp. vinegar
1 tbsp. salad mustard	Salt and pepper to taste
1/4 tsp. pepper	Pimento strips
1/4 c. mayonnaise	1/2 to 1 c. hot broth

Cut the eggs in half lengthwise. Remove yolks and sieve. Add the mustard, pepper, mayonnaise and vinegar and mix until smooth. Add salt and pepper and mix. Refill whites and garnish with pimento. Arrange in chafing dish. Add enough broth just to cover bottom of dish and cover. Keep warm.

Mrs. Delores McEnearey, Maxwell AFB, Alabama

SHIRRED EGGS MONTMORENCY

4 tbsp. butter	1/2 c. light cream
1/4 c. chopped onions	1/2 tsp. dill powder
2 tbsp. minced anchovies	6 hard-cooked eggs, quartered
1 c. tomato sauce	1 tbsp. chopped parsley

Melt the butter in blazer pan over low heat. Add the onions and anchovies and cook until onions are tender. Add the tomato sauce, cream and dill and cook for 1 to 2 minutes or until sauce boils, stirring occasionally. Place pan over hot water. Place eggs in sauce and heat through. Sprinkle with parsley. 4 servings.

Mrs. Laura Gwyer, Prattville, Alabama

chafing dish desserts

When you want the perfect ending for a simple supper . . . when you come home from the movies . . . when friends drop in for an evening visit . . . serve a chafing dish dessert. These quick-and-easy desserts are among the most eye-appealing of all chafing dish recipes.

Think of how your family and guests would enjoy Rio Banana Flambe, a flaming dessert that reflects the Spanish influence in America's Southland. Two tart and tangy flavors mix in Apples Poached in Orange Juice — and the delicious result is indescribable! That typical southern fruit — the peach — takes on new dimensions when it is served in Brandy Peaches.

The ultimate chafing dish dessert is pancakes. Many hostesses recommend that you prepare the pancakes in advance — they can even be frozen. When you are ready to serve dessert, bring the prepared pancakes to the table. Then dazzle your family and guests by preparing the dessert sauce in front of their admiring eyes. You'll find a marvelous recipe for a traditional pancake dessert, Crepes Suzette, in the following pages.

This and other carefully-developed, home-tested original recipes are awaiting you in the section that follows. As you read through them, imagine the delighted expressions on your family's faces as you serve them a chafing dish dessert — tonight!

RIO BANANA FLAMBE

3 tbsp. butter or margarine	6 med. bananas, sliced lengthwise
3/4 c. (packed) brown sugar	2 tbsp. brandy
1/4 c. dark rum	Vanilla ice cream

Melt the butter and sugar in a chafing dish and add the rum. Place bananas in dish and simmer for about 7 minutes. Heat the brandy and ignite. Pour over bananas and stir gently until flame burns out. Serve over ice cream. 6 servings.

Mrs. H. B. Smith, Miami, Florida

CHAFING DISH FIGS IN CREAM

1/2 lb. dried figs	1/2 c. heavy cream
1/2 c. cognac	1/16 tsp. salt
1/2 c. whole filberts	Macaroons
1/4 c. butter	

Place the figs in a bowl. Pour the cognac over figs and marinate overnight. Drain and reserve cognac. Stuff the figs with filberts. Melt the butter in blazer pan over hot water. Add the figs and cook until tender. Pour reserved cognac over figs and ignite. Let flame die down, then stir in cream and salt. Heat through. Serve with macaroons. 6 servings.

Mrs. Pat Green, Montgomery, Alabama

CERISE NOIR

1 12-oz. jar red currant jelly	Slivered almonds
3 tbsp. lemon juice	3/4 c. brandy
1 can pitted cherries, drained	Vanilla ice cream

Melt the jelly in a chafing dish and add the lemon juice. Stuff cherries with almond slivers and add to chafing dish. Add 1/4 cup brandy and simmer for 6 to 8 minutes. Add remaining brandy and ignite. Spoon over ice cream while flaming. 10-12 servings.

Mrs. Herbert Dean, Albany, Georgia

FRESH APPLE CREPES

4 med. apples	2 tbsp. butter
3/4 c. water	1/8 tsp. salt
3/4 c. sugar	

Pare and core the apples and slice in thick slices. Combine the apples, water, sugar, butter and salt in a saucepan and bring to a boil. Reduce heat and simmer until apples are tender. Drain apples and reserve syrup. Keep apples and reserved syrup warm.

Cheese Sauce

1 3-oz. package cream cheese	1/2 c. shredded Cheddar cheese
	1/2 c. sour cream

Soften the cream cheese in a mixing bowl. Add the Cheddar cheese and beat until smooth. Blend in the sour cream and set aside.

Crepes

2 eggs	2 tsp. sugar
2/3 c. milk	1/4 tsp. salt
2 tbsp. melted butter	1/8 tsp. cinnamon
1/2 c. sifted all-purpose flour	Butter

Beat the eggs well in a mixing bowl. Add the milk and butter and mix. Sift the flour, sugar, salt and cinnamon together. Add to milk mixture and beat until smooth. Butter a 6-inch skillet and heat until very hot. Pour the batter, 2 tablespoons at a time, into the skillet, tilting skillet to cover bottom. Cook until lightly browned. Turn and brown on other side. Stack Crepes until ready to use. Place 3 or 4 apple slices on each Crepe and top with 1 tablespoon Cheese Sauce. Roll Crepes and place in single layer in a chafing dish. Pour reserved apple syrup over Crepes and heat. Serve 2 filled Crepes per serving and top each serving with a dollop of Cheese Sauce.

Fresh Apple Crepes (page 96)

APPLES POACHED IN ORANGE JUICE

6 to 8 apples	1/2 c. (packed) light brown sugar
Orange juice	Dash of nutmeg
1 tbsp. Cointreau	Dash of mace

Peel the apples and cut each apple into 6 wedges. Place in blazer pan and add enough orange juice to cover. Cover blazer pan and place over water pan. Cook until apples are just tender. Add the Cointreau and sprinkle with sugar and spices. Keep warm.

Mrs. Alex Moore, Portsmouth, Virginia

SKILLET APPLE SLICES

3 lge. apples	1/2 c. heavy cream
3 tbsp. butter	1/8 tsp. cinnamon
1/4 c. sugar	Dash of salt
1/2 c. muscatel	

Pare and core the apples. Cut in thin slices. Place in blazer pan with butter and sprinkle with 2 tablespoons sugar. Cover and cook over moderate heat for about 5 minutes, turning apples once or twice. Add the muscatel and cover. Simmer until apples are tender. Place blazer pan over hot water and keep warm. Whip the cream with remaining sugar, cinnamon and salt until stiff and serve with apples. 4-5 servings.

Mrs. G. H. Downey, Wilson, North Carolina

CHERRY-ALMOND JUBILEE

1/4 c. slivered almonds	1 1/2 tsp. cornstarch
2 tbsp. butter	1/4 tsp. almond extract
1 1-lb. can red pitted dessert cherries	Vanilla ice cream

Saute the almonds in butter in a saucepan until golden brown. Drain the cherry juice into a blazer pan or saucepan and blend in the cornstarch. Cook over medium heat until thickened and clear, stirring constantly. Add the cherries and almonds and heat through. Stir in almond extract and place over hot water. Serve warm over ice cream.

Photograph for this recipe on page 94.

LIME CREPES

1 qt. strawberries, hulled and halved	1/4 c. butter or margarine
12 Crepes	1/2 c. (packed) brown sugar
	1/3 c. lime juice

Lime Crepes (page 98)

1/2 c. orange liqueur	**1 tsp. grated lime rind**
1 c. heavy cream, whipped	

Place about 6 strawberry halves in a row in the center of each Crepe and roll Crepes. Set aside. Heat the butter in chafing dish over canned heat flame and stir in the sugar. Add the lime juice, stirring constantly, and bring to a boil. Simmer for 2 minutes. Add the Crepes and heat through, basting with sauce frequently. Sprinkle Crepes with liqueur and ignite. Shake pan until flames burn out. Serve Crepes with whipped cream and sprinkle with grated rind.

Crepes

2/3 c. sifted all-purpose	**1 1/2 c. milk**
flour	**2 tbsp. melted butter or**
1 tbsp. sugar	**margarine**
1/2 tsp. salt	**1 tbsp. brandy**
3 eggs	**Oil**
3 egg yolks	

Sift the flour, sugar and salt together. Beat the eggs and egg yolks well in a medium bowl. Add the milk, flour mixture, butter and brandy and beat until smooth. Cover and refrigerate for 2 hours. Add the batter, about 1/4 cup at a time, to an oiled 8-inch skillet and tip and tilt the skillet so that the batter covers the bottom. Cook until lightly browned. Turn and brown other side. Stack Crepes between waxed paper until ready to fill.

CRIMSON CRANBERRY FLAMBE

1 1/2 c. sugar	1/4 to 1/2 c. brandy
1 c. water	Coconut ice cream
2 c. fresh cranberries	

Mix the sugar and water in a blazer pan and bring to a boil. Add the cranberries and simmer for about 5 minutes or until skins pop. Pour brandy over top and ignite. Ladle sauce over scoops of ice cream. 6-8 servings.

Mrs. Arthur Kier, Ft. George G. Meade, Maryland

CHOCOLATE PEARS

3/4 c. sugar	1 1/2 tsp. cocoa
1 tbsp. cornstarch	1 c. water
1/4 tsp. cloves	1 tbsp. butter
1 tsp. cinnamon	Pear halves

Combine first 6 ingredients in blazer pan of chafing dish and place over low heat. Simmer until mixture is thickened. Add the butter and pear halves and simmer until pear halves are soft. Place blazer pan over hot water. Garnish pears with whipped cream, if desired.

Mrs. Marlene Couverchal, Montgomery, Alabama

STUFFED PEARS MILANESE

6 lge. firm pears	1/4 lb. toasted almonds, ground
1/2 c. powdered sugar	1/4 tsp. almond extract
4 maraschino cherries, finely chopped	1/2 c. dry sherry

Cut the pears in half lengthwise and remove cores. Blend remaining ingredients except sherry and place in cavities of pears. Arrange pears in chafing dish and pour sherry over pears. Cover and cook for 15 minutes or until pears are tender. Keep warm over hot water.

Mrs. Jack Ripley, Williamsburg, Kentucky

PEACH-MINCEMEAT FLAMBE

1 pkg. mincemeat	1/4 c. brandy
1 can peach halves, drained	

Prepare mincemeat according to package directions. Place peach halves in a blazer pan and fill each cavity with mincemeat. Place blazer pan over hot water and heat for 5 to 10 minutes or until peaches are heated through. Heat the brandy and ignite. Pour flaming brandy over peaches.

Mrs. Victor Mandeville, Little Rock, Arkansas

BRANDY PEACHES

4 tbsp. butter	4 fresh peaches, peeled
1/2 c. sugar	6 tbsp. brandy
1/4 c. water	

Melt the butter and sugar in blazer pan of chafing dish and blend well. Stir in the water. Add the peaches and place blazer pan over water pan. Cook for 30 to 35 minutes, turning peaches frequently. Add the brandy and keep warm. 4 servings.

Mrs. Michael York, Silver Springs, Maryland

ORANGE-PEACH CRUMBLE

6 c. sliced fresh peaches	1/4 tsp. salt
6 tbsp. frozen orange juice	1/2 tsp. cinnamon
concentrate, thawed	1/4 tsp. nutmeg
1 c. (packed) brown sugar	1/3 c. soft butter or
1/2 c. all-purpose flour	margarine
1/2 c. rolled oats	Orange-Cream Topping

Place the peaches in a 2-quart chafing dish blazer pan and sprinkle with undiluted orange concentrate. Mix the brown sugar, flour, oats, salt, cinnamon and nutmeg in a bowl and cut in butter until crumbly. Sprinkle over peaches. Place blazer pan over low flame and cook for 20 minutes or until the peaches are tender. Serve warm with Orange-Cream Topping.

Orange-Cream Topping

1 c. heavy cream	2 tbsp. orange juice concentrate, thawed

Whip the cream in a bowl until stiff. Fold in undiluted orange concentrate.

Orange-Peach Crumble (above)

BUTTERSCOTCH CREAM

2 tbsp. butter
2 c. brown sugar
2 3/4 c. milk
1/2 c. flour

2 eggs
Sliced bananas
Nuts

Combine the butter, brown sugar and 3/4 cup milk in blazer pan of chafing dish and cook over low heat for 6 minutes, stirring constantly. Mix the flour, eggs and remaining milk and beat until smooth. Add to cooked mixture gradually, stirring, and cook until thick, stirring frequently. Place blazer pan over water and keep warm. Top with bananas and nuts before serving.

Mrs. Lucian Henning, Princeton, West Virginia

COTTAGE PUDDING WITH BLUEBERRY SAUCE

1/4 c. shortening
1 c. sugar
1 egg
1/4 tsp. lemon extract
1 3/4 c. all-purpose flour
2 1/2 tsp. baking powder
1/2 tsp. salt
1/2 tsp. cinnamon

1/2 tsp. nutmeg
2/3 c. milk
1 No. 2 can blueberry pie
   filling
1/4 c. honey
1/4 c. butter
3 tbsp. lemon juice

Cream the shortening and sugar in a bowl. Add egg and lemon extract and beat well. Sift the flour, baking powder, salt and spices together and add to creamed mixture alternately with milk, beating well after each addition. Place in paper-lined 8 x 8 x 2-inch pan. Bake in 350-degree oven for 35 minutes or until done. Cut into 3-inch squares. Combine the pie filling, honey, butter and lemon juice in blazer pan of chafing dish and heat. Place over water pan and keep warm. Spoon sauce over warm pudding squares. 6-8 servings.

Hazel Wimer, Hightown, Virginia

CREPES SUZETTE

3 eggs
1 c. milk
3/4 c. unsifted flour
Sugar

1/4 tsp. salt
1/2 c. margarine
1 tsp. grated orange peel
1/3 c. Cointreau

Beat the eggs and milk in a small mixing bowl, then beat in the flour, 1 tablespoon sugar and salt. Pour the batter, 2 tablespoons at a time, onto a lightly greased 5 or 6-inch skillet. Cook over medium heat until lightly browned and top is bubbly. Turn and brown other side. Fold each crepe in quarters and set aside. Melt the margarine in a large skillet or chafing dish and add 2/3 cup sugar and grated orange peel. Cook until mixture bubbles. Place folded crepes in sauce and cook for 5 minutes, or until sugar starts to caramelize, basting crepes occasionally with sauce. Pour Cointreau over top and ignite. Serve immediately. 16 crepes.

Photograph for this recipe on cover.

FLAMING STRAWBERRY OMELET

4 eggs, separated	1 tbsp. butter
1/4 tsp. salt	2 c. sliced sweetened
1 tbsp. sugar	strawberries
4 tbsp. rum	

Beat the egg yolks with salt in a mixing bowl until light. Add the sugar and 1 tablespoon rum and mix well. Beat the egg whites until stiff and fold into the yolk mixture. Melt the butter in a chafing dish. Pour egg mixture into pan and cook over medium heat, pulling egg mixture from sides into middle until set. Fold in half and sprinkle with additional sugar. Ignite remaining rum in a ladle and pour over omelet slowly. Serve flaming with strawberries. 4 servings.

Flaming Strawberry Omelet (above)

Shrimp Stroganoff (page 112)

chafing dish seafood and poultry

When you are serving a main course from your chafing dish, southern homemakers recommend that you choose a recipe featuring seafood or poultry. Both these foods cook quickly — a must for successful chafing dish cookery!

In this section, homemakers from Maryland to Texas share some of their best chafing dish seafood and poultry recipes with you — dishes like Crab Imperial . . . Lobster Newberg . . . and Oysters Jambalaya. These are the party recipes served in homes throughout the Southland.

Some of the very finest recipes are those using shrimp — a traditional southern seafood. Shrimp Creole Delight is an up-to-date version of a dish which dates from the earliest settlement of the Gulf coast region.

Another traditional southern food favorite is chicken — and this section contains recipes just made to be cooked or served in chafing dishes. Captain's Chicken is a recipe that was originated in the South, while Chafing Dish Tetrazzini is a southern version of an Italian dish. Both recipes share the delicious taste and eye-appealing color so important to a successful party dish.

At your next gathering, serve one of these seafood or poultry chafing dish recipes. Then sit back and listen to your family and guests praise your cooking — and your style of serving from a chafing dish!

CRAB IMPERIAL

1 green pepper, chopped	1 tbsp. Worcestershire sauce
1 tbsp. butter	1 tsp. salt
1 sm. can pimentos	1/4 tsp. dry mustard
6 tbsp. mayonnaise	1 lb. back fin crab meat

Saute the green pepper in butter in a saucepan for 1 minute. Drain and chop the pimentos. Add the mayonnaise, Worcestershire sauce, salt, mustard and green pepper and mix well. Stir in the crab meat and place in chafing dish over hot water. Cook over low heat for 25 minutes. 6 servings.

Mrs. Mary S. Cooley, Suffolk, Virginia

CRAB JACQUES

2 tbsp. butter	Salt and pepper to taste
3 tbsp. flour	2 tbsp. sherry
1 c. milk	1 lb. crab meat
1/2 c. grated Cheddar cheese	

Melt the butter in blazer pan of chafing dish. Blend in the flour. Add the milk and cook, stirring constantly, until thick. Add the cheese, salt, pepper, sherry and crab meat and cook until cheese is melted. Place over hot water. Serve crab mixture in pastry shells or on toast. Juice of 1/2 lemon may be substituted for sherry.

Mrs. W. G. Waters, Savannah, Georgia

CRAB BALLS IN SAUCE

1 med. onion, minced	1/3 c. milk
5 tbsp. olive or cooking oil	1/2 tsp. Worcestershire sauce
4 tbsp. flour	1 tsp. chopped parsley
2 c. tomato sauce	1 5 1/2-oz. can crab meat
1/4 tsp. allspice	3/4 c. cracker crumbs
Salt and pepper	1 egg
1/8 tsp. paprika	

Cook the onion in 1/4 cup oil in a blazer pan until golden. Stir in 2 tablespoons flour. Add the tomato sauce and allspice and bring to a boil, stirring constantly. Cook for 3 minutes, then add salt and pepper to taste. Heat remaining oil in a saucepan. Add remaining flour, 1/8 teaspoon salt and paprika and mix well. Add the milk and cook until thick, stirring constantly. Remove from heat and add the Worcestershire sauce and parsley. Drain and flake the crab meat. Add to sauce and mix well. Chill. Shape into balls and roll in crumbs. Beat the egg with 2 tablespoons water and dip the crab balls in egg mixture. Roll in crumbs again.

Fry in deep fat at 375 degrees until brown and drain on paper towels. Place blazer pan over water pan and place crab balls in tomato sauce in blazer pan. Cook until heated through.

Mrs. Paulyne D. Murphy, Dam Neck, Virginia

ROCK LOBSTER BUFFET

5 9-oz. packages frozen rock lobster-tails	1/4 c. brandy 1 c. tomato sauce
2 tbsp. butter	1 pt. canned tomatoes,
2 tbsp. olive oil	chopped
1 clove of garlic, chopped	1 c. white wine
2 onions, minced	1/2 tsp. crumbled basil
2 carrots, minced	Salt and pepper to taste

Cut frozen lobster-tails into 1-inch crosswise slices, shell and all, with a sharp knife. Heat the butter and oil in blazer pan of chafing dish over low heat. Add the garlic, onions and carrots and saute for 5 minutes. Add the lobster pieces and remaining ingredients and cover tightly. Cook, stirring occasionally, for about 20 minutes. Season with salt and pepper. Place over hot water to keep warm. 12 servings.

Rock Lobster Buffet (above)

FILLET OF FLOUNDER

1 lb. flounder fillets	1/2 c. grated sharp Cheddar
Salt and pepper to taste	cheese
1 tbsp. butter or margarine	Chopped parsley to taste
1 tbsp. flour	Paprika to taste
1/3 c. milk or light cream	

Place the fillets in a greased shallow casserole and add salt and pepper. Bake at 375 degrees for 15 minutes, then place in a chafing dish. Melt the butter in a saucepan and stir in the flour. Add the milk slowly and cook until thickened, stirring constantly. Add the cheese and stir until melted. Spread over fillets and sprinkle with parsley and paprika. Place over hot water and cook for 15 minutes longer. Keep hot. 4 servings.

Mrs. R. D. Cox, Raleigh, North Carolina

SPICED FISH

1 lb. fish fillets	1/4 c. vinegar
1/2 tsp. cayenne pepper	2 cloves of garlic, minced
1/4 tsp. pepper	3 onions, chopped
1 tsp. curry powder	2 tbsp. margarine
1/2 tsp. sugar	3 tomatoes, sliced
1 tsp. salt	1 tbsp. lime juice

Cut the fish in bite-sized pieces. Mix the cayenne pepper, pepper, curry powder, sugar, salt and vinegar and add the fish. Marinate for several hours. Fry the garlic and onions in margarine in blazer pan of chafing dish over low heat until golden. Add the fish and fry until brown. Add tomatoes and cover. Simmer for about 20 minutes. Add lime juice and place over hot water. Keep hot. Serve with rice. 4 servings.

Mrs. Guy Harvey, Princeton, Florida

CRUNCHY SALMON SCALLOP

2 tbsp. finely chopped onion	2 c. milk
1/4 c. chopped green pepper	1 1-lb. can salmon
3 tbsp. butter	1 tbsp. lemon juice
3 tbsp. flour	2 hard-cooked eggs, sliced
1 tsp. salt	2 c. corn flakes
1/8 tsp. pepper	

Cook the onion and green pepper in butter in a saucepan until tender and stir in the flour, salt and pepper. Add the milk and stir constantly over low heat until thick. Drain the salmon and remove bones. Arrange in a greased chafing dish and sprinkle with lemon juice. Add the eggs and half the corn flakes. Cover with sauce and top with remaining corn flakes. Heat over low heat until bubbly, then place over hot water. Keep hot.

Mrs. Miller F. Jones, Winston-Salem, North Carolina

SALMON JUBILEE

1 can mushroom soup	1 tbsp. chopped parsley
1/4 c. milk	1 tsp. minced onion
2 c. canned salmon, drained	1 c. grated Cheddar cheese
1/2 tsp. salt	1 c. toasted bread crumbs
1/4 tsp. pepper	

Combine the soup and milk in blazer pan over hot water and heat through. Flake the salmon and add to soup mixture. Add the salt, pepper, parsley and onion and stir until mixed. Stir in the cheese and cover with crumbs. Cook for 30 minutes. 4 servings.

Mrs. Opal Freeman, Pine Bluff, Arkansas

LOBSTER NEWBERG

2 tbsp. butter	Salt and pepper to taste
2 c. cooked lobster	3 egg yolks, beaten
1/2 c. sherry	1 tbsp. brandy (opt.)
1/2 c. cream	

Melt the butter in a blazer pan and add the lobster and sherry. Cook for 10 minutes. Add the cream and cook until mixture bubbles. Add the salt and pepper. Stir small amount of lobster mixture into egg yolks, then stir back into lobster mixture. Cook until thickened. Place over hot water. Add the brandy and keep warm.

Russell W. Raifsnider, Fairfax, Virginia

COQUILLE ST. JACQUES

1 vegetable bouillon cubes	1 c. instant nonfat dry milk
1 c. boiling water	4 tbsp. butter
1/2 tsp. salt	3 tbsp. flour
1/4 tsp. pepper	3 tbsp. grated Parmesan
1/4 tsp. crushed bouquet	cheese
garni	2 tbsp. dry bread crumbs
1 1/2 lb. scallops	1/4 c. chopped parsley
1 6-oz. can sliced mushrooms	

Dissolve the bouillon cube in water in a saucepan and stir in the salt, pepper and bouquet garni. Cut the scallops in 1-inch cubes and add to bouillon mixture. Cover and cook over low heat for 8 minutes. Drain the scallops and reserve liquid. Drain the mushrooms and add liquid to reserved scallop liquid. Add enough water to make 1 1/2 cups liquid and stir in the milk. Melt 3 tablespoons butter in a blazer pan and stir in the flour. Add milk mixture and cook, stirring, until thickened and smooth. Stir in the scallops, mushrooms and cheese and place over hot water. Melt remaining butter and mix with bread crumbs. Sprinkle over scallop mixture and sprinkle parsley over top.

Edith Mason, Baltimore, Maryland

OYSTERS BLANDINE

1 tbsp. garlic juice	4 c. buttered toasted bread
1 tbsp. onion juice	cubes
1 tbsp. Worcestershire sauce	2 qt. oysters, drained
1 tsp. salt	1/2 c. butter
1 tsp. pepper	1/2 c. grated American
1 c. milk	cheese (opt.)

Mix the garlic juice, onion juice, Worcestershire sauce, salt, pepper and milk. Place layers of bread cubes, oysters, and butter in a blazer pan until all ingredients are used. Pour milk mixture over all. Place blazer pan over hot water and cook for 30 minutes. Reduce heat and keep warm. Sprinkle cheese over top. 6-8 servings.

Mrs. Russell O. Behrens, Apalachicola, Florida

OYSTER JAMBALAYA

3 tbsp. salad oil	Chopped onion tops to taste
2 tbsp. flour	Chopped parsley to taste
2 c. cold water	1/2 tsp. red pepper
1/2 c. diced celery	1 pt. oysters
1/2 c. diced onion	2 c. cooked rice
1 tbsp. salt	

Heat the oil in blazer pan of chafing dish over low heat. Add the flour and cook, stirring constantly, until brown. Add remaining ingredients except oysters and rice and cook until celery is tender. Add the oysters and cook until edges curl. Add rice and place over hot water.

Mrs. Roy Waitz, Alexandria, Louisiana

SHRIMP BALLS

1 lb. shelled shrimp, cleaned	1 tsp. sherry flavoring
10 water chestnuts, chopped	1/2 tsp. salt
fine	1 egg, slightly beaten
1 tbsp. cornstarch	

Chop the shrimp and mix with water chestnuts. Add the cornstarch, sherry flavoring and salt and stir in the egg. Shape into balls. Fry in deep fat until golden brown. Drain on paper towel and place in blazer pan over hot water. 12-15 servings.

Mrs. C. E. McKeown, Gore, Virginia

SHRIMP CREOLE DELIGHT

5 tbsp. shortening	1/2 c. minced onion
1/4 c. flour	1/2 c. minced parsley
1 tbsp. minced garlic	2 c. water

1 lb. peeled cleaned shrimp
Salt to taste
2 bay leaves

1/4 tsp. cayenne pepper
2 tbsp. tomato paste

Melt the shortening in blazer pan of chafing dish. Add flour and brown. Add the garlic, onion and parsley and cook, stirring constantly, for 2 minutes. Add the water gradually, stirring constantly. Bring to a boil and add shrimp and remaining ingredients. Cover and simmer for 20 minutes. Place over hot water and serve over rice. 4 servings.

Mrs. James D. Arnold, Vicksburg, Mississippi

CURRIED SEAFOOD

1   9-oz. package frozen
    lobster-tails
1   7-oz. package frozen
    deveined shrimp
1/4 c. butter
1/4 c. chopped onion
1 tsp. curry powder

1 tbsp. all-purpose flour
1 can cream of mushroom soup
1 c. milk
1 c. sour cream, at room
    temperature
1   6-oz. package frozen
    crab meat, thawed

Cook the lobster and shrimp according to package directions, then cut in large pieces. Melt the butter in a blazer pan. Add the onion and curry powder and saute until onion is tender. Blend in the flour. Add the soup, then stir in milk gradually. Bring to a boil and reduce heat. Cook for 2 minutes. Stir in the sour cream, lobster and shrimp. Drain the crab meat and add to lobster mixture. Heat to serving temperature. Do not boil. Place on a stand over low flame. Serve lobster mixture over rice. 8 servings.

Curried Seafood (above)

SHRIMP STROGANOFF

3 tbsp. butter	1 10 1/2-oz. can beef
1/2 c. chopped onion	broth
1 sm. clove of garlic,	1 2-oz. can sliced
minced	mushrooms
1/4 c. all-purpose flour	2 c. cooked shrimp
1 tsp. salt	1 c. yogurt, at room
1/2 tsp. dillweed	temperature

Melt the butter in a chafing dish blazer pan. Add the onion and garlic and saute until onion is tender. Stir in the flour, salt and dillweed. Remove from heat and stir in the beef broth and mushrooms with liquid gradually. Cook over medium heat, stirring constantly, until thickened. Add the shrimp and cook over low heat for 5 to 10 minutes. Stir in the yogurt and heat to serving temperature. Do not boil. Place blazer pan over hot water. Serve shrimp mixture over rice or noodles. 4-6 servings.

Photograph for this recipe on page 104.

CHICKEN CHARLOTTE LOUISE

1 fryer, disjointed	1 can orange juice concentrate
Salt and pepper to taste	Chopped parsley to taste
1/4 lb. margarine or butter	2 sm. oranges, sliced thin

Season the chicken with salt and pepper and place, skin side up, in baking pan. Melt the margarine and add the orange juice concentrate and parsley. Spoon over chicken. Bake at 350 degrees for about 45 minutes. Place in chafing dish over hot water. Add orange slices and cook for 20 minutes.

Mrs. J. Julian Conlon, Charleston, South Carolina

CAPTAIN'S CHICKEN

1/2 c. flour	1/2 c. chopped green pepper
1 tsp. salt	1 garlic clove, minced
1/4 tsp. pepper	1 1/2 tsp. curry powder
1 fryer, disjointed	1/2 tsp. thyme
1/4 c. butter	1 20-oz. can tomatoes
2 tbsp. instant minced onion	3 tbsp. seedless raisins
1 tbsp. dried parsley flakes	

Combine the flour, salt and pepper and roll chicken in flour mixture. Brown in butter in a skillet. Add the onion, parsley flakes, green pepper, garlic, curry powder and thyme and cook until green pepper is tender. Add the tomatoes and bring to a boil. Cover and simmer until chicken is tender. Add the raisins and place in chafing dish over hot water. Keep hot. Serve with rice.

Ann Elsie Schmetzer, Madisonville, Kentucky

CHICKEN SUPREME IN RAISIN SAUCE

1 4-lb. fryer	2 stalks celery, sliced
1 tsp. paprika	1 onion, sliced
1/2 tsp. instant coffee	1 lge. carrot, sliced
1 1/2 tsp. seasoned salt	1/2 c. seedless raisins
1/4 c. flour	Salt
1/4 c. shortening	Pepper to taste
1 10 1/2-oz. can bouillon	

Cut the chicken in serving pieces. Mix the paprika, instant coffee, seasoned salt and flour and coat the chicken with flour mixture. Brown in shortening in a skillet over low heat on both sides and drain off excess fat. Add bouillon, celery, onion and carrot and cover tightly. Simmer for about 1 hour or until chicken is tender. Remove chicken to chafing dish and keep warm. Strain mixture in skillet and discard vegetables. Skim off excess fat from liquid and add enough water or additional bouillon, if necessary, to make 1 1/4 cups liquid. Add to chicken. Add the raisins, salt and pepper and heat for 5 to 10 minutes longer. Thicken sauce with small amount of cornstarch mixed with cold water, if desired. 4 servings.

Chicken Supreme in Raisin Sauce (above)

CREAMED CHICKEN OVER CROUTONS

2 1/2 c. buttered toast cubes	1 can cream of celery soup
2 c. grated cheese	Milk
2 c. diced cooked chicken	3 eggs, beaten

Place alternate layers of bread cubes, cheese and chicken in buttered blazer pan. Mix the soup with enough milk to make 2 cups liquid and stir in the eggs. Pour over chicken mixture and cover. Place over water pan and cook for 10 minutes. Keep hot.

Mrs. Ed Kemper, Arlington, Virginia

NEW DELHI CHICKEN

10 slices bacon	Chopped parsley to taste
1/4 c. butter	Pinch of thyme
1 3-lb. chicken	1 bay leaf
1 tbsp. flour	Salt and pepper to taste
1 c. sweet red wine	15 sm. onions, peeled
1 c. chicken stock	1 tbsp. cornstarch

Cut the bacon in small pieces and fry until crisp. Drain. Melt the butter in a blazer pan. Cut the chicken into serving pieces and fry in butter until golden brown on all sides. Remove from blazer pan. Stir flour into butter in blazer pan. Add the wine, stock, parsley, thyme, bay leaf, salt, pepper, onions and bacon and bring to a boil, stirring constantly. Reduce heat and add the chicken. Cover and cook over low heat for about 1 hour or until chicken is tender. Mix the cornstarch with 1 tablespoon water and stir into sauce. Cook for several minutes longer or until slightly thickened. Place blazer pan over hot water.

Mrs. Ruby Bonelli, Vicksburg, Mississippi

DEVILED CHICKEN

1 2 to 3-lb. fryer, disjointed	1 can consomme
1 tsp. salt	1/4 c. water
Dash of pepper	1 tbsp. prepared mustard
1/4 c. salad oil	1 tbsp. Worcestershire sauce
3 tbsp. flour	1 tbsp. catsup
	1/4 tsp. paprika

Season the chicken with salt and pepper and brown in oil in blazer pan over medium heat. Remove chicken. Add flour to oil and stir over low heat until smooth. Stir in the consomme and water. Mix the mustard, Worcestershire sauce, catsup and paprika and add to consomme mixture. Return chicken to blazer pan. Cover and simmer for 45 minutes or until chicken is tender, spooning sauce over chicken frequently. Place blazer pan over hot water. Serve the chicken and sauce on rice.

Mrs. C. W. Handly, Dallas, Texas

CHAFING DISH CHEDDAR CHICKEN

4 oz. broad noodles	1 c. cheese soup
1 4 1/2-oz. jar mushrooms	1 c. finely crushed cheese
2 1/2 c. diced cooked chicken	crackers
1 tbsp. instant minced onion	2 tbsp. melted butter
1 c. milk	

Cook the noodles according to package directions and place in a chafing dish over hot water. Combine the mushrooms and chicken and place on noodles. Mix the onion, milk and soup and pour over chicken mixture. Combine the cracker crumbs and butter and sprinkle over top. Cook over low heat until heated through.

Ida McGee, Mount Airy, North Carolina

CHAFING DISH TETRAZZINI

1 1/2 c. noodles	1/2 c. cream of mushroom
1 1/2 c. diced celery	soup
1 tsp. chopped green pepper	3/4 c. drained canned
1/2 c. chopped onion	tomatoes
1 clove of garlic, chopped	Salt and pepper to taste
1 tbsp. chopped parsley	3/4 c. grated sharp cheese
3 c. chicken broth	2 tbsp. bread crumbs
2 c. chopped cooked chicken	

Cook the noodles, celery, green pepper, onion, garlic and parsley in broth until noodles are tender. Add remaining ingredients and mix well. Place in blazer pan and place blazer pan over hot water. Cover and heat thoroughly. 6-8 servings.

Mrs. C. G. Clark, Alexander City, Alabama

CHICKEN ARROZ CALDO

1 fryer	2 tbsp. shortening
1 1-in. cube ginger	3 tbsp. soy sauce
1 clove of garlic, chopped	1 1/2 c. rice
fine	6 c. boiling water
1 sm. onion, chopped	2 green onions, chopped

Cut the chicken in serving pieces. Pare and slice the ginger. Saute with garlic and onion in shortening in a blazer pan over low heat until onion is tender. Add the chicken, soy sauce, rice, water and onions and simmer until chicken is tender. Place blazer pan over hot water.

Mrs. Leonor L. Lapid, Elizabeth City, North Carolina

Party Chicken Livers (below)

PARTY CHICKEN LIVERS

2 lb. chicken livers	1/4 c. finely chopped onion
1/4 c. butter or margarine	1/4 c. sherry
1 1/2 tsp. salt	1/2 tsp. hot sauce

Cut the chicken livers in half. Heat the butter in a large skillet. Add half the chicken livers and sprinkle with 3/4 teaspoon salt. Brown quickly on both sides, then place in a chafing dish. Add remaining chicken livers to skillet and sprinkle with remaining salt. Brown and place in chafing dish. Add onion to skillet and cook until tender but not brown. Stir in the sherry and hot sauce and heat, stirring occasionally, until all drippings are loosened from the skillet. Pour into chafing dish. Cook, stirring frequently, for about 10 minutes or until livers are done. May serve with rice or egg noodles.

CHICKEN LIVERS IN SOUR CREAM

4 tbsp. butter	1 tsp. salt
3 tbsp. flour	1/4 tsp. pepper

1 lb. chicken livers, cut in half	1 c. sour cream
1/2 lb. fresh mushrooms, sliced	1 tsp. paprika

Melt the butter in blazer pan over low heat. Mix the flour, salt and pepper and coat the livers with flour mixture. Brown the livers in the butter. Add the mushrooms and cover the pan. Cook for about 5 minutes or until mushrooms are tender. Stir in the sour cream and paprika and place blazer pan over hot water. Cook until heated through. 4-6 servings.

Mrs. Lorraine Richiarelli, Birmingham, Alabama

CHAFING DISH CHICKEN AND DUMPLINGS

1 hen	1 bay leaf
2 stalks celery and leaves	3 tbsp. flour
Few sprigs of parsley	3 tbsp. margarine or butter
1 sm. onion	Salt and pepper to taste

Place the chicken in a kettle and cover with water. Add the celery, parsley, onion and bay leaf and bring to a boil. Reduce heat and simmer until the chicken is tender. Remove chicken from the broth and cool. Remove skin. Remove chicken from bones in large pieces. Strain and cool the broth. Remove excess fat. Blend flour and margarine in blazer pan over low heat. Add 3 cups broth to the flour mixture gradually and cook, stirring, until thickened and smooth. Season with salt and pepper. Add the chicken and heat until bubbling.

Dumplings

1 c. flour	2 tsp. baking powder
Salt to taste	Milk

Combine flour, salt and baking powder in a bowl and add enough milk to make a soft dough. Drop by spoonfuls into chicken mixture and cook for 15 to 20 minutes. Do not stir. Place blazer pan over hot water and keep warm.

Mrs. A. B. Dean, St. Petersburg, Florida

TURKEY FEUILLETE

3 tbsp. butter or margarine	Salt and pepper to taste
3 tbsp. flour	3 c. cooked turkey
3/4 c. chicken stock	1/4 c. dry vermouth
3/4 c. milk	6 patty shells

Melt the butter in blazer pan over low heat and stir in the flour. Add the chicken stock, milk, salt and pepper and cook, stirring frequently, until thickened. Add the turkey and vermouth and stir until blended. Heat through, then place blazer pan over hot water. Spoon into patty shells just before serving. 6 servings.

Mrs. A. L. Monroe, Toccoa, Georgia

chafing dish beef, pork and lamb

Mouth-watering, eye-appealing main dishes are the center of attraction when you prepare beef, pork, and lamb chafing dish recipes. Southern women who combine the heartiness of these meats with the elegance of chafing dish cookery know that they have a winning combination.

Because *Southern Living* readers enjoy preparing such dishes, they have spent time and energy developing a number of delicious recipes — recipes like Beef Short Ribs with Raisin Sauce in which the flavors mingle and the textures of the two main ingredients complement each other in a great blend — and a wonderful main dish! There are other beef recipes awaiting your discovery in the pages that follow — Belgian Meatballs . . . Beef Stroganoff . . . Creole Steak to name just a few.

Pork and lamb come in for their share of attention with recipes such as Pork Cubes with Pineapple. And a southern way of preparing ham — by stuffing it — takes the spotlight with Stuffed Chafing Dish Ham Rolls. Still another flavor treat awaits your family when you serve Lamb Curry, a hot and hearty dish adapted especially for American tastes by a creative southern homemaker.

These are just some of the recipes you'll discover in the pages that follow — recipes you'll want to serve at your next party or on any occasion when you are looking for an extra-special, family-approved chafing dish meal!

International Ripe Olive Meatballs (below)

INTERNATIONAL RIPE OLIVE MEATBALLS

2 c. canned pitted ripe olives	2 tbsp. chopped parsley
1 lb. ground beef	2 tbsp. chopped mint
1/2 c. chopped onion	1 1/2 tsp. salt
1/2 c. pine nuts	2 tbsp. cooking oil
1 egg	International Sauce

Drain the ripe olives. Mix the ground beef, onion, nuts, egg, parsley, mint and salt and shape small amount of beef mixture around ripe olives to form balls. Brown in hot oil in a skillet. Place in a chafing dish. Serve with International Sauce for dipping.

International Sauce

1 onion, minced	1 1/2 tsp. chili powder
1 green pepper, chopped	1/2 tsp. salt
1 clove of garlic, minced	1/2 c. tomato juice
2 tbsp. butter	1/2 c. beef broth
1 tbsp. flour	

Cook the onion, green pepper and garlic in the butter in a saucepan until green pepper is limp. Blend in the flour, chili powder and salt. Add the tomato juice and beef broth gradually and cook until thickened.

BARBECUED BEEF BUNS

1/4 c. vinegar	4 tbsp. mustard
1/4 c. sugar	1 tsp. salt
1/2 c. butter	2 thick slices lemon
1/4 tsp. pepper	1 c. catsup
1/4 tsp. cayenne pepper	3 tsp. Worcestershire sauce
2 onions, sliced	4 c. cubed cooked beef
1 1/2 c. water	4 pitted ripe olives

Combine the vinegar, sugar, butter, peppers, onions, water, mustard, salt and lemon in a blazer pan and bring to a boil over high heat. Reduce heat and simmer for 20 minutes. Add the catsup, Worcestershire sauce and beef and simmer for 15 minutes longer. Chop the olives and stir into beef mixture. Place blazer pan over water pan and keep hot. Serve beef mixture on buns.

Debbie Harper, Williamsburg, Virginia

BEEF CONTINENTAL

1 4-oz. can sliced mushrooms	1 can tomato soup
1 1/2 c. cubed cooked beef	1/2 soup can water
1 onion, chopped	2 tbsp. chopped parsley
1/8 tsp. leaf thyme	1/2 med. bay leaf
2 tbsp. butter or margarine	2 c. cooked noodles or rice

Drain the mushrooms. Cook the beef, mushrooms, onion and thyme in butter in a blazer pan until onion is tender. Add soup, water, parsley and bay leaf and cover. Cook over low heat for 20 minutes, stirring occasionally . Remove bay leaf and place blazer pan over hot water. Serve beef mixture over noodles. 6 servings.

Mrs. Dorothy G. Morrow, Waco, Texas

BONGSOR BEEF CURRY

2 lb. cubed boneless beef chuck	1/4 tsp. ground coriander
1/4 c. seasoned flour	1/2 tsp. ground cumin
2 lge. onions, sliced	1/2 tsp. turmeric
4 tbsp. margarine	1/8 tsp. cayenne pepper
1 c. boiling water	1/2 c. tomato juice

Sprinkle the beef with seasoned flour. Cook beef and onions in margarine in chafing dish blazer pan over medium heat until brown. Add the water, coriander, cumin, turmeric and cayenne pepper and bring to a boil. Reduce heat and cover. Simmer for 1 hour and 30 minutes or until beef is tender. Stir in tomato juice and place pan over hot water. Serve on rice with condiments of chutney, raisins, coconut, peanuts and cashews.

Mrs. Estelle Shalla, Bay City, Texas

BEEF WITH DUMPLINGS

1 1 1/2-lb. can beef stew
1 c. drained cooked mixed
    vegetables
2 tbsp. instant minced onion

1 c. tomato juice or tomato
    sauce
1 c. prepared biscuit mix
1/3 c. milk

Combine first 4 ingredients in chafing dish blazer pan and mix well. Place over medium heat and cover. Heat to serving temperature, stirring frequently. Mix the biscuit mix and milk until dry ingredients are moistened and drop by spoonfuls onto hot beef mixture. Cover. Cook over low heat for about 15 minutes or until dumplings are done. Place blazer pan over hot water and keep warm. 2 to 3 servings.

Mrs. Grace Murphy, Eufaula, Alabama

SOY-BEEF WITH GREEN PEAS

1 lb. beef, cut in cubes
2 med. onions, chopped
1 c. chopped celery
2 tbsp. shortening
1/2 c. rice
1 can chicken-noodle soup
1 can cream of mushroom soup

4 tbsp. soy sauce
1 tsp. salt
1/4 tsp. pepper
1 can green peas or green
    beans
2 c. water

Brown the beef, onions and celery in shortening in chafing dish blazer pan over low heat. Add remaining ingredients and mix well. Cook over low heat for 1 hour or until beef is tender. Place blazer pan over hot water.

Mrs. James E. Spurlin, Chickasha, Oklahoma

BEEF SHORT RIBS WITH RAISIN SAUCE

3 lb. beef short ribs
3 tbsp. shortening
Salt and pepper to taste
1 onion, chopped
1/2 c. brown sugar
1 tsp. dry mustard
1/2 c. raisins

1 tbsp. flour
2 tbsp. vinegar
2 tbsp. lemon juice (opt.)
1/4 tsp. grated lemon rind
1 bay leaf
1 1/2 c. water

Cut the ribs in serving pieces. Brown in hot shortening in a skillet, then pour off drippings. Season ribs with salt and pepper. Add onion. Combine remaining ingredients in a saucepan and bring to a boil. Pour over ribs and cover tightly. Cook over low heat for about 2 hours or until beef is tender, adding water, if needed. Thicken the sauce, if desired. Place the ribs mixture in a blazer pan and place blazer pan over hot water. 6-8 servings.

Mrs. Fred Hill, Centerville, Texas

SHORT RIBS WITH VEGETABLES

2 lb. short ribs	2 cloves of garlic, minced
1/2 c. flour	1 tbsp. Worcestershire sauce
1 tbsp. salt	4 carrots, sliced
1/4 tsp. pepper	2 onions, sliced
1 stick margarine	2 potatoes, cubed
1 1-lb. can tomatoes	Parsley sprigs

Cut the ribs in serving pieces. Combine the flour, salt and pepper. Dredge ribs with flour mixture and brown in margarine in a skillet. Add tomatoes, garlic and Worcestershire sauce and cover. Simmer for 1 hour. Add the carrots, onions and potatoes and simmer for 45 minutes longer, adding water, if needed. Place ribs mixture in a chafing dish over hot water and garnish with parsley.

Mrs. Anna Canalle, Winchester, Virginia

STUFFED ROUND STEAK

4 slices bacon, diced	5 slices cubed steak
1 onion, chopped	1/2 tsp. salt
1 1/2 c. toasted bread cubes	1/8 tsp. pepper
2 tbsp. minced parsley	1 c. bouillon
1/2 tsp. celery salt	1 8-oz. can tomato sauce
1/4 tsp. sage	

Saute the bacon with onion in a skillet until onion is tender. Mix in bread cubes, parsley, celery salt and sage. Season steak with salt and pepper and spread each slice with stuffing. Roll up and secure with toothpicks. Place in blazer pan and pour bouillon over steak rolls. Cover and simmer for 30 minutes. Add the tomato sauce and cover. Simmer for 30 minutes or until steak is done. Garnish with parsley. Place blazer pan over water pan and keep hot.

Nancy Cross, Harrison, Arkansas

STEAK ALGERIENNE

1 lb. round steak	1/4 c. salad oil
5 tbsp. soy sauce	1 sm. onion, chopped
1 tsp. sugar	1/2 tsp. ground ginger
2 lge. tomatoes	2 tsp. cornstarch
2 lge. green peppers	

Slice steak as thin as possible and cut in 1-inch pieces. Mix 1/4 cup soy sauce and sugar and pour over steak. Marinate for 30 minutes. Cut tomatoes and green peppers in 1-inch cubes. Heat oil in chafing dish blazer pan over high heat. Add the onion, ginger and green peppers and cook for 3 minutes over medium heat. Add the steak and marinade and cook for 3 minutes. Add the tomatoes. Mix the cornstarch and remaining soy sauce and stir into steak mixture. Cook for 3 minutes longer. Keep hot over water until ready to serve. Serve on rice. 4 servings.

Mrs. Ralph Willey, Sr., Enfield, North Carolina

CREOLE STEAK

1 1/2 lb. round steak,	2 slices onion
1 in. thick	1/2 tsp. salt
2 tbsp. bacon fat	1/8 tsp. pepper
2 c. canned tomatoes	1/8 bay leaf
3 whole cloves	

Cut the steak in serving pieces and brown in the bacon fat in a blazer pan. Add the tomatoes and remaining ingredients and cook over low heat for 1 hour or until steak is tender. Remove cloves and bay leaf. Place blazer pan over hot water.

Catherine Whilten, Grayson, Louisiana

MADEIRA STEAK

1/2 c. self-rising flour	1 can mushroom soup
1/2 tsp. pepper	1 soup can milk
1 tsp. paprika	1/2 soup can water
6 slices tenderized steak	4 tbsp. Madeira
1/2 c. oil	

Mix the flour, pepper and paprika in a paper bag. Add the steak and shake well. Brown the steak in oil in blazer pan of chafing dish over medium heat. Mix remaining ingredients and pour over steak. Cook for 45 minutes or until steak is done. Place over hot water.

Mrs. George F. Turner, Timberville, Virginia

BELGIAN MEATBALLS

1 lb. hamburger	1/8 tsp. pepper
2 tbsp. finely chopped onion	1/2 c. milk
2 tbsp. chopped green pepper	1 egg
1/4 c. cornmeal	1/4 c. flour
1 tsp. chili powder	1/4 c. shortening
1 tsp. dry mustard	1 1/2 c. cooked tomatoes
1 tsp. salt	

Combine the hamburger, onion, green pepper, cornmeal, seasonings, milk and egg in a bowl and blend thoroughly. Form into 12 balls and roll in flour. Brown in hot shortening in chafing dish blazer pan over medium heat. Drain off excess fat. Add remaining flour to pan and stir well. Add the tomatoes and cover. Cook for 35 minutes or until meatballs are done. Place over hot water. 6 servings.

Mrs. Richard D. Massey, Avant, Oklahoma

GRECO

1 onion, chopped	1 can mushrooms, drained
1 green pepper, chopped	1 lb. ground beef

Salt and pepper to taste
3 c. cooked shell macaroni
3 sm. cans tomato sauce

1 can white cream-style corn
Parmesan or sharp Cheddar
  cheese, grated

Cook the onion, green pepper and mushrooms in small amount of fat in chafing dish over low heat until tender. Add the ground beef and cook until beef loses red color. Add the salt, pepper, macaroni, tomato sauce and corn and mix well. Sprinkle generously with cheese. Cook over low heat for 25 to 30 minutes. Place over water pan and keep hot. 10-12 servings.

Mrs. W. C. Niceley, Fountain City, Tennessee

RIPE OLIVE-BEEF TACOS

1 lb. ground lean beef
Cooking oil
3/4 c. chopped onion
1 clove of garlic, minced
1 tsp. salt
2 finely chopped canned
  green chilies
1 8-oz. can tomato sauce

1 tall can pitted ripe
  olives
8 corn tortillas
Shredded lettuce
Shredded Monterey Jack
  cheese
Sliced avocado
Sliced cherry tomatoes

Cook the ground beef in 1 tablespoon cooking oil in chafing dish blazer pan over medium heat until partially done. Add the onion and garlic and cook until beef is brown. Add salt, chilies and tomato sauce. Drain and chop the olives and add to beef mixture. Cook over low heat for about 5 minutes. Add tomatoes and keep hot. Fry the tortillas lightly in oil in a skillet. Fold in half, holding with fork to shape, and drain well. Fill tortillas with ripe olive mixture and add the lettuce, cheese and avocado as desired.

Ripe Olive-Beef Tacos (above)

BEEF STROGANOFF

1/2 c. chopped onions	1 can cream of chicken soup
2 lb. ground round steak	1 4-oz. can mushroom stems
3 tbsp. margarine	and pieces
Salt and pepper to taste	2 8-oz. cartons sour cream

Saute the onions and ground steak in margarine in chafing dish blazer pan over medium heat until brown. Season with salt and pepper and stir in the soup. Add mushroom pieces and liquid and simmer for 25 minutes. Place blazer pan over hot water. Fold sour cream into soup mixture and keep hot. Serve over rice.

Billye Short, Hurst, Texas

VEAL PARMESAN

1/4 c. flour	Oil
1/2 c. grated Parmesan cheese	1 lge. onion, thinly sliced
1/2 tsp. salt	1 green pepper, thinly sliced
Dash of pepper	1/2 c. barbecue sauce
6 veal steaks	1 8-oz. can tomato sauce
1 egg, beaten	Dash of garlic salt

Combine the flour, cheese, salt and pepper. Dip veal in egg, then in seasoned flour. Brown in small amount of oil in blazer pan of chafing dish over medium heat. Drain off oil. Add the onion and green pepper. Combine remaining ingredients and pour over veal mixture. Sprinkle with additional cheese. Cover and cook over medium heat for 35 minutes or until veal is done. Place over hot water. 6 servings.

Pearl Scott, Gainesville, Florida

BRAISED PORK STEAKS

1 1/2 tbsp. tomato sauce	2 pork steaks
1 tbsp. lemon juice	1/2 sm. onion, sliced
1/4 tbsp. mustard	1 c. water
1/2 tsp. Worcestershire sauce	

Combine the tomato sauce, lemon juice, mustard and Worcestershire sauce and rub on both sides of steaks. Brown in small amount of fat in blazer pan of chafing dish over medium heat. Top with onion slices and add the water. Cover and cook over medium heat for 30 minutes or until steaks are tender. Place blazer pan over hot water. 2 servings.

Betty Ann Robinson, Erin, Tennessee

PORK CHOPS AND BROCCOLI

1 pkg. frozen broccoli	Salt and pepper to taste
4 to 6 pork chops	2 tbsp. shortening

1 can mushroom or celery soup	1/2 c. water
	1/2 c. grated cheese

Cook the broccoli according to package directions until partially done and drain. Sprinkle the pork chops with salt and pepper and brown in shortening in chafing dish blazer pan on both sides. Pour soup and water over pork chops and add broccoli. Sprinkle cheese over top and cook over low heat until chops are tender. Place blazer pan over hot water to keep warm.

Mrs. Esther Stewart, Vian, Oklahoma

LEMON-SMOTHERED CHOPS

2 lb. thick pork chops	1 green pepper, cut in rings
2 unpeeled lemons, sliced	1 tsp. salt
1 lge. onion, sliced	2 c. tomato juice

Brown the pork chops in small amount of fat in a blazer pan and drain off fat. Top with lemon slices, onion, green pepper and salt and add tomato juice. Cover and cook for about 45 minutes or until pork chops are tender. Place blazer pan over water pan and keep hot.

Mrs. Hilda Burdine, Somerset, Kentucky

PORK CHOP-SWEET POTATO DINNER

6 pork chops	6 slices pineapple
Salt and pepper to taste	12 lge. prunes
3 lge. sweet potatoes, sliced	12 whole cloves
Lemon juice	1/2 c. pineapple juice

Season the pork chops with salt and pepper and brown in small amount of fat in blazer pan of chafing dish over medium heat. Sprinkle sweet potatoes with lemon juice and place on pork chops. Add pineapple slices. Remove pits from prunes and insert cloves. Place in blazer pan and pour pineapple juice over all ingredients. Cover and simmer for about 45 minutes. Place blazer pan over water pan and keep hot.

Mrs. Nina Parker, Williamston, North Carolina

SPANISH PORK CHOPS

6 pork chops, cut 1 in. thick	1 tbsp. dry mustard
1 tbsp. shortening	2 tbsp. vinegar
1 tbsp. salt	1/3 to 1/2 c. water
1/8 tsp. pepper	1 tbsp. sugar
1/4 c. catsup	

Brown the pork chops in shortening in chafing dish blazer pan. Pour off excess fat. Season chops with salt and pepper. Mix catsup and mustard and spread on chops. Combine the vinegar, water and sugar and pour around chops. Cover tightly and simmer for 45 minutes or until chops are done. Place over hot water. 5-6 servings.

Mrs. E. L. Allen, Kenton, Tennessee

PORK CUBES WITH PINEAPPLE

1 1/2 lb. boneless pork	1/4 c. water
Seasoned flour	1 green pepper, cut in strips
2 tbsp. salad oil	1 12-oz. jar pineapple
1/2 c. barbecue sauce	preserves
1/4 c. vinegar	

Cut the pork in 1-inch cubes and coat with seasoned flour. Brown in oil in chafing dish blazer pan over low heat. Add the barbecue sauce, vinegar and water and cover. Simmer for 45 minutes. Add green pepper and preserves and cook for 15 minutes longer. Place blazer pan over water pan and keep hot. 6 servings.

Mrs. Pat Allen, Little Rock, Arkansas

SWEET AND SOUR PORK SUPREME

1 1/2 lb. lean pork	1 c. apricot preserves
Seasoned flour	1/2 c. sliced dill pickles
1/2 c. water	1/2 c. pineapple cubes
1/4 c. vinegar	1/2 c. cubed tomato
2 tbsp. soy sauce	

Cut the pork in cubes and coat with seasoned flour. Brown in small amount of fat in chafing dish blazer pan over low heat. Stir in the water, vinegar and soy sauce and cover. Simmer for 45 minutes. Add the preserves, dill pickles, pineapple and tomato and simmer for 15 minutes. Place over hot water. Serve pork mixture over rice, if desired. 4 servings.

Mrs. Barbara C. Reeves, Gainesville, Florida

COUNTRY HAM WITH RAISIN SAUCE

4 to 6 slices country-cured ham	1 tsp. whole cloves

Place the ham and cloves in a skillet and add enough water to cover ham. Bring to a boil and reduce heat. Cover and cook for about 40 minutes or until ham is tender. Drain.

Raisin Sauce

1/2 c. seedless raisins	1 tbsp. cornstarch
1/4 c. chopped citron (opt.)	1 tbsp. butter
1 c. boiling water	1/2 tsp. lemon juice
3/4 c. sugar	

Mix the raisins, citron and water in a blazer pan and simmer until raisins are tender. Sift sugar and cornstarch together. Add to raisin mixture and mix well. Cook, stirring constantly, for 10 minutes. Place over hot water. Add the butter, lemon juice and ham and keep hot.

Mrs. Phil Ingle, Granite Falls, North Carolina

MINIATURE TART SHELLS WITH HAM

2 tbsp. oil
1 clove of garlic
1 c. chopped ham
1 c. chopped mushrooms

1 tbsp. chopped parsley
Salt and pepper to taste
24 miniature tart shells

Heat the oil in a small chafing dish over low heat. Add the garlic and cook for 3 minutes. Remove garlic and discard. Add the ham, mushrooms, parsley and seasonings and saute for 4 minutes. Place chafing dish over hot water. Place ham mixture in tart shells just before serving.

Mrs. Tom Gardner, Ozark, Alabama

LOUISIANA YAMS AND HAM BALLS

1 1/2 lb. ground cooked ham
1 c. soft bread crumbs
1 egg, slightly beaten
1 med. onion, finely chopped
1/8 tsp. pepper
1/4 c. butter or margarine
1 1/2 tbsp. prepared mustard

3/4 c. (firmly packed) brown
 sugar
3/4 c. vinegar
2 1-lb. cans yams,
 drained
1 1/2 tbsp. cornstarch

Combine the ham, crumbs, egg, onion and pepper and mix well. Shape into 18 balls. Melt the butter in chafing dish blazer pan. Add ham balls and cook over low heat until browned on all sides. Combine the mustard, sugar, vinegar and 1 1/4 cups water and add to ham balls. Add the yams and cook, covered, over low heat for 15 minutes. Remove yams and ham balls to a dish. Blend the cornstarch with 1/4 cup water and add to sauce. Bring to a boil, stirring constantly. Return yams and ham balls to sauce in blazer pan. Place over water pan and keep warm.

Louisiana Yams and Ham Balls (above)

STUFFED CHAFING DISH HAM ROLLS

1   12-oz. package frozen rice
    with peas and mushrooms
1/2 c. grated sharp American
    process cheese

8 slices boiled ham
1 10-oz. package frozen
    onions in cream sauce
1 env. white sauce mix

Prepare the rice according to package directions, omitting Parmesan cheese. Stir in the American cheese. Spoon 1/4 cup on each ham slice and roll as for jelly roll. Prepare onions according to package directions. Prepare white sauce mix in blazer pan over low heat according to package directions. Add the onion mixture and mix well. Place ham rolls in sauce and cover. Heat through. Place over hot water. 4 servings.

Mrs. L. S. Lawrence, Abilene, Texas

CHAFING DISH SAUSAGE WITH SPAGHETTI

1 sm. package spaghetti
1 lb. bulk pork sausage
2/3 c. diced cheese
2 tbsp. butter

Salt and pepper to taste
1 6-oz. can spaghetti
sauce

Prepare the spaghetti according to package directions and drain. Cook the sausage in a chafing dish blazer over low heat until brown. Add the spaghetti, cheese, butter, salt, pepper and spaghetti sauce and mix. Place over hot water to keep warm.

Mrs. Blanche Jeffries, Horse Cave, Kentucky

RAISIN LAMB CURRY WITH PERSIAN RICE

1 tbsp. curry powder
1 tbsp. butter
1 med. onion, sliced
2 med. stalks celery, sliced
1 1/2 lb. boneless lean lamb
1 14-oz. can chicken broth

1 tsp. garlic salt
2/3 c. seedless raisins
1 1/2 tbsp. cornstarch
2 tbsp. water
Persian Rice

Combine the curry powder, butter, onion and celery in chafing dish blazer pan and cover. Cook over moderate heat for several minutes or until vegetables wilt. Cut the lamb in small cubes and add to onion mixture. Add the broth and garlic salt and cover tightly. Simmer for 1 hour to 1 hour and 30 minutes or until lamb is tender. Add the raisins and cornstarch mixed with water and cook over low heat for 15 minutes longer. Place over hot water. Serve over Persian Rice.

Persian Rice

2 tbsp. butter
1 c. rice
1 c. orange juice

1 1/2 c. water
1 tsp. salt
1/2 c. seedless raisins

1/4 c. slivered toasted almonds	1/4 tsp. grated orange peel
	1 tbsp. chopped parsley

Combine the butter and rice in a skillet and cook over moderate heat, stirring, until light brown. Stir in the orange juice, water, salt and raisins and cover tightly. Simmer for about 15 minutes or until rice has absorbed all liquid and is tender, stirring once or twice during first 5 minutes of cooking. Remove from heat and fluff rice with a fork. Add the almonds, orange peel and parsley. 4-6 servings.

Photograph for this recipe on page 118.

FRIED LAMB AND RICE

2/3 c. chopped onion	3 tbsp. oil
1/4 c. diced green pepper	3 c. cooked rice
1 clove of garlic, minced	2 c. cubed cooked lamb

Saute the onion, green pepper and garlic in oil in a blazer pan until tender. Add the rice and lamb and cook until browned. Add just enough boiling water to cover bottom of pan. Keep hot over water.

Mrs. H. F. Benson, Hereford, Texas

LAMB CURRY

2 lb. ground lamb	1 tsp. basil
1/2 c. chopped onion	1/2 c. chopped celery
1 c. canned tomatoes	1/2 lb. fresh mushrooms,
1 tsp. oregano	sliced

Brown the ground lamb and onion in small amount of fat in chafing dish blazer pan over low heat. Add the tomatoes and herbs and heat thoroughly. Add the celery and mushrooms. Cover and cook over low heat for 30 to 40 minutes. Place blazer pan over hot water. May serve with saffron rice.

Mrs. Annie Lee A. Glover, Lynchburg, South Carolina

LAMB PATTIES WITH CURRANT SAUCE

1 1/2 lb. ground lamb	1/4 tsp. marjoram
1 c. soft bread crumbs	1 egg, well beaten
1/4 c. milk	1/2 c. red currant jelly
1 tsp. salt	1/2 tsp. grated orange rind

Combine first 6 ingredients and shape in 3/4-inch thick patties. Brown on both sides in blazer pan of chafing dish over medium heat. Heat the jelly in a saucepan until melted and add orange rind. Pour over patties and place blazer pan over hot water.

Myrtle M. Stafford, West Liberty, Kentucky

Gingered Lamb and Vegetables Orientale (138)

oriental cookery

For spectacular and unusual entertaining, southern hostesses take their cue from the Orient. Using versatile Japanese and Chinese utensils and cooking methods, women throughout the South create memorable party dishes for every occasion.

With the *wok,* a Chinese frying pan, they create stir-fry dishes while their families and guests watch in amazement. Tender-crisp vegetables mingle their flavors with those of meat strips and carefully seasoned sauces in wok-fried dishes such as Gai Lo Mein.

And on Japanese *hibachis, Southern Living* readers create everything from piping-hot cocktail tidbits to absolutely delicious main dishes like Skewered Shrimp.

Also from Japan comes *tempura,* a way of frying bits of meat, seafood, or vegetables in a crisp, feather-light batter. Shino Tempura captures all the flavor excitement of this unusual method of cooking.

With these recipes are hints for bringing oriental cookery successfully into your home. As you read through these pages, you'll be excited at the many possibilities for brand-new cooking and dining treats. Try one of these recipes soon and bring a subtle touch of the Orient to your dining table!

oriental cookery

KNOW-HOW

From two of the world's most ancient cuisines have come cooking methods and utensils used by American homemakers to bring sparkle to their own cookery. Three of these — the utensils known as the *wok* and the *hibachi* and the cooking method called *tempura* — are featured in this *Fondue and Buffet Cookbook* because they can add so much to any buffet gathering.

The *wok* comes from China. It is a rounded pan with sloping sides used to cook food by the stir-fry method. The word "wok" is from the Cantonese dialect of China and simply means "cooking vessel." In former times, the wok was placed over a charcoal brazier which provided sufficient heat for cooking. Today, a metal ring can be bought to fit under the wok and over conventional electric or gas stove burners.

A gas stove is preferred to an electric one as a heat source because the heat level must be quickly controlled. However, a wok can be lifted from an electric stove to cool the temperature.

Woks were traditionally made from iron but today are made from stainless steel and aluminum. A new wok must be seasoned before using. To season, wash the wok and rinse thoroughly. Dry, and then place over a low flame on the stove burner until all liquid has evaporated. Raise the flame to medium heat and wipe the inside of the wok thoroughly, using a pad that has been saturated with vegetable oil. Repeat the wiping process three or four times until no trace of dirt comes off on the paper. Once the wok has been seasoned, it should never be scoured or washed with soap. After using, fill with water and let sit until the food residue has worked loose. Stubborn spots can be cleaned with salt. An iron wok should always be dried over a low flame as it will rust if any water is left after washing and drying.

The most versatile size is 12 to 14 inches in diameter, which is sufficient for most family and party cooking. Cooking in a wok requires mastery of two techniques — chopping all foods to be cooked beforehand and cooking them quickly at very high temperatures. Only small quantities of food should be prepared at one time: about one pound of meat is the maximum. The entire surface of a wok is used for cooking, and the handles will become heated. So, heavy cooking mitts are a must.

All meats and vegetables are chopped before cooking begins. The oil is heated, and the meat and tougher vegetables are added. Then come the more delicate vegetables, the liquid, and the seasonings. Toss them with a light motion as you would salad vegetables — and keep them in constant movement. Cooking in a wok should take no more than five minutes, and the food should be served immediately as it becomes greasy if it is allowed to stand.

Tempura is a Japanese way of cooking food in fat. It is an adaptation of the Portuguese deep-fat frying which was brought to Japan by explorers and missionaries during the sixteenth and seventeenth centuries. Although Westerners were expelled from Japan in 1638, the tempura method of cooking remained and later became one of the best-known features of Japanese cuisine.

Foods that can be successfully cooked in this manner include shrimp, chicken, fish, and virtually all vegetables except watery ones such as radishes. The secret of tempura cooking lies in the oil mixture and in the batter. Fine tempura cooks spend long hours developing just the right blend of oils — the one we suggest is about 70 percent vegetable oil and 30 percent sesame oil.

The batter may be any one of a number of variations of an egg - ice - water - flour mixture. The batter is kept ice-cold (usually by setting it over a bowl of crushed ice). While the oil heats to a temperature of 375 degrees, the food to be fried is lightly coated with the icy batter. As soon as the oil reaches the right temperature, six or eight bits of coated food are put into the pan. The batter literally explodes on contact with the oil, and the food inside is cooked by a combination of steam and hot fat.

A key to successful tempura cookery is to keep the fat clean. Japanese cooks do this by skimming it with a net after each batch of food has been cooked and served. A good tempura cook can serve ten people continuously — and keep the oil clean at the same time!

Another notable Japanese contribution to western cookery is the *hibachi,* a small charcoal brazier which is remarkably suited for indoor cooking. Ranging in size from tiny ones three inches square (great for cooking spectacular appetizers) to huge four-burner ones, hibachis offer a size for every need.

To use indoors, choose a well-ventilated room — a sun porch, perhaps. By carefully adjusting the draft doors on the hibachi, you'll find that you can get just the degree of heat you need. For a fun party, try letting your guests prepare their own skewers of meat, seafood, and vegetables and cooking them over an indoor hibachi.

Chinese Pepper Steak (below)

CHINESE PEPPER STEAK

1 lb. round or flank steak	1/4 tsp. pepper
1/4 c. corn oil	1/4 tsp. ginger
1 clove of garlic	1 tbsp. cornstarch
1/2 c. coarsely chopped onion	1 c. stock or bouillon
2 c. green pepper cubes	1 tbsp. soy sauce
1 tsp. salt	Cooked rice

Cut the steak diagonally across the grain in thin slices, then cut in 2-inch long strips. Heat the corn oil in Chinese wok or blazer pan of chafing dish over medium heat. Add garlic and cook for 3 minutes. Remove garlic and discard. Add steak to oil and cook over medium heat, stirring frequently, until browned. Add the onion, green pepper, salt, pepper and ginger and cook over medium heat, stirring constantly, for 3 minutes or until vegetables are just tender. Blend cornstarch with stock and soy sauce and stir into steak mixture. Bring to a boil and cook, stirring constantly, until thickened. Keep hot. Serve over rice. 4 servings.

YAKITIZERS

2 lb. top sirloin steak, 1 in. thick	1 tsp. ground ginger
1/2 c. soy sauce	1/4 tsp. pepper
1/4 c. brown sugar	1 clove of garlic, minced
2 tbsp. salad oil	Canned water chestnuts, halved

Freeze steak partially and slice in thin strips. Combine the soy sauce, brown sugar, oil, ginger, pepper and garlic in a deep bowl and mix well. Add the steak and water chestnuts and mix. Let stand for 2 hours at room temperature. Drain steak and water chestnuts and reserve marinade. Thread beef strips on metal skewers accordion-style and add a water chestnut. Broil over hot coals of hibachi for 5 to 6 minutes, turning frequently and basting with marinade. 6-8 servings.

Mrs. Doris Adams, Atlanta, Georgia

SUKIYAKI

1 lb. beef sirloin or rib	1/4 c. unsulphured molasses
2 tbsp. cooking oil	2 tbsp. soy sauce
1 lge. green pepper, cut in thin strips	1 tsp. lemon juice
	1/2 tsp. salt
2 green onions, thinly sliced	1 tsp. monosodium glutamate
	1 tsp. ginger
1/2 c. thin diagonally sliced celery	1/2 c. water
	2 tsp. cornstarch

Cut the beef in thin strips and brown in hot oil in large tempura pan or skillet. Add the green pepper, green onions and celery and cook for 3 to 5 minutes, stirring frequently. Stir in the molasses, soy sauce, lemon juice, salt, monosodium glutamate and ginger. Blend water and cornstarch and stir into beef mixture. Cover and simmer for 5 minutes. Serve with hot, cooked rice. 4 servings.

Sukiyaki (above)

CHOP SUEY

1 lb. pork	**1 tsp. salt**
2 tbsp. shortening	**1/8 tsp. pepper**
1 c. chopped celery	**4 tbsp. soy sauce**
1 c. sliced onions	**1 No. 2 can bean sprouts**

Cut the pork in 1/2-inch cubes and brown in shortening in Chinese wok or blazer pan of chafing dish over medium heat. Add the celery, onions, salt, pepper, soy sauce and bean sprouts and liquid. Cook, stirring frequently, for 15 minutes. Keep warm.

Tommy Bo Hannon, Lake Wales, Florida

GAI LO MEIN

1 lb. fresh pork, diced	**1 c. chopped onions**
2 tbsp. oil	**1/2 c. bean sprouts**
1/3 c. flour	**3 c. sliced celery**
2 c. beef bouillon	**1 c. slivered blanched**
3 tbsp. soy sauce	**almonds**
3/4 c. mushrooms	

Brown the pork in oil in Chinese wok or blazer pan of chafing dish over medium heat. Sprinkle with flour and mix well. Stir in the bouillon and soy sauce and heat through. Add the mushrooms, onions, bean sprouts, celery and almonds and cover. Simmer for 30 minutes, stirring occasionally. Keep warm. Serve over hot, buttered noodles. 6 servings.

Mrs. Bertie Knapp, Lexington, Kentucky

WON TON FRY

6 c. flour	**1/2 c. chopped celery**
1/2 c. water	**1/2 c. bean sprouts**
1 egg	**2 tbsp. soy sauce**
1 1/2 c. cooked ground pork	**1/4 tsp. salt**
1 tbsp. chopped green onion	**1/4 tsp. pepper**

Mix the flour with water and egg and knead on a floured surface until smooth. Roll out very thin and cut in 2-inch squares. Combine remaining ingredients. Place 1 teaspoon pork mixture in center of each square. Moisten edges, fold over and seal. Fry in 2 inches of hot fat in an electric skillet until brown. Drain and serve.

Becky Elizabeth Wallace, Bartlesville, Oklahoma

GINGERED LAMB AND VEGETABLES ORIENTALE

2 lb. boned leg of lamb	**1 8-oz. can water**
1/2 c. peanut or salad oil	**chestnuts**
6 c. lengthwise-sliced onions	**1 5-oz. can bamboo**
3 4-oz. cans whole	**shoots**
mushrooms	**1/2 c. soy sauce**

| 3 to 4 tbsp. shredded gingerroot | 2 tbsp. cornstarch |
| | Chow mein noodles |

Cut the lamb in thin strips and brown in 1/4 cup oil in a Chinese wok or blazer pan of chafing dish over high heat, stirring constantly. Remove lamb. Add remaining oil and heat. Brown the onions in oil. Drain the mushrooms and reserve liquid. Drain and slice the water chestnuts. Drain the bamboo shoots. Add the mushrooms, lamb, water chestnuts, bamboo shoots, soy sauce and gingerroot to onions and heat through, stirring constantly. Dissolve the cornstarch in 1/4 cup cold water and add reserved mushroom liquid and enough water to make 2 1/4 cups liquid. Blend with lamb mixture and cover. Cook over medium heat, stirring constantly, until thickened and clear. Keep hot. Serve with chow mein noodles. Two to 3 teaspoons ground ginger may be substituted for gingerroot. 10-12 servings.

Photograph for this recipe on page 132.

LAMB KABOBS

1/2 tsp. hot sauce	1/2 tsp. salt
1/2 c. salad oil	1/8 tsp. basil
1/4 c. lime or lemon juice	2 lb. boneless lamb shoulder
1/4 c. red wine (opt.)	1 green pepper
1 tbsp. onion juice	3 tomatoes, quartered
1 tsp. dry mustard	12 sm. whole onions

Blend the hot sauce, salad oil, lime juice, wine and onion juice in a bowl. Add the mustard, salt and basil and mix well. Cut the lamb in 1 1/2-inch cubes and add to oil mixture. Refrigerate for 5 hours or overnight. Cut the green pepper in 1-inch pieces. Drain the lamb. Place the lamb and vegetables alternately on skewers. Broil or grill on hibachi 4 inches from heat for about 10 minutes on each side. 6 servings.

Lamb Kabobs (above)

TAIWAN RICE WITH CHICKEN

1 c. diced cooked chicken	1/4 c. minced green pepper
1/2 tsp. salt	1/2 c. thinly sliced green
1 tbsp. soy sauce	onions
1/3 c. vegetable oil	1/4 c. thinly sliced celery
2 c. rice	1/2 c. finely shredded lettuce
2 1/2 c. chicken broth	2 eggs, slightly beaten

Combine the chicken, salt and soy sauce in a mixing bowl and let stand for 15 minutes. Heat the oil in a Chinese wok or blazer pan of chafing dish over medium heat. Add the rice and cook, stirring, until golden. Reduce heat and stir in the broth and chicken with marinade. Cover and simmer for 15 minutes or until rice is tender. Remove cover. Add remaining ingredients except lettuce and eggs and cook until liquid is absorbed. Push rice mixture to side of wok. Add eggs and cook, stirring, until almost set. Stir into the rice mixture. Stir in the lettuce and serve at once. 6-8 servings.

Mrs. Harry Allen, Montgomery, Alabama

CHINESE SHRIMP

1 tbsp. salad oil	2 tbsp. soy sauce
1 8-oz. package frozen	1 tbsp. cornstarch
snow peas	2 tbsp. cold water
3/4 c. chicken broth	1 4 1/2-oz. can shrimp,
2/3 c. sliced water chestnuts	drained
1/4 tsp. salt	

Heat oil in Chinese wok or skillet over burner. Add the snow peas and heat until thawed, separating peas. Stir in the chicken broth, water chestnuts, salt and soy sauce and cover. Cook for 2 minutes, stirring frequently. Combine the cornstarch and water and stir into water chestnut mixture. Cook, stirring constantly, for 2 minutes or until thickened and clear. Add the shrimp and mix. Heat through. 2-3 servings.

Mrs. Marty Varley, Birmingham, Alabama

SHINO TEMPURA

Peeled cleaned fresh shrimp	1 c. sifted flour
Asparagus spears	1 c. ice water
Sweet potatoes	1 egg, lightly beaten
Mushrooms	1/2 tsp. sugar
Green beans	1/2 tsp. salt
Salad oil	

Dry shrimp and vegetables well. Slice vegetables or cut into strips, if needed. Fill electric skillet 1/2 full with salad oil and heat to 365 degrees. Combine the flour, ice water, egg, 2 tablespoons oil, sugar and salt and stir just until mixed. Stir in 1 ice cube. Dip shrimp and vegetables in cold batter. Fry in oil in the skillet until light brown and drain. Serve with condiments of grated fresh gingerroot, equal parts grated turnip and radish mixed and prepared mustard mixed with soy sauce.

Mrs. M. J. Blount, Padukah, Kentucky

Hibachi Rock Lobster Kabobs (below)

HIBACHI ROCK LOBSTER KABOBS

8 frozen rock lobster-tails
2 unpeeled navel oranges,
   quartered
8 cling peach halves
1/2 c. melted butter or
   margarine

1/3 c. dry sherry
Juice of 1 lemon
1 6-oz. can frozen
   concentrated pineapple-
   orange juice, thawed

Thaw the lobster-tails. Cut underside membràne with scissors and remove lobster meat carefully from shell in 1 piece. Thread meat lengthwise on a skewer with an orange quarter and a peach half. Combine remaining ingredients and brush on kabobs. Place on hibachi grill 6 inches above gray coals and broil until lobster meat becomes opaque and lightly browned, turning kabobs and brushing with sauce several times. Serve with remaining sauce.

SKEWERED SHRIMP

1/2 c. chili sauce
1/4 c. salad oil
2 tbsp. dark corn syrup
2 tbsp. vinegar
1/2 clove of garlic, minced

1/2 tsp. salt
1/4 tsp. pepper
2 lb. peeled cleaned shrimp
2 lemons, cut in wedges

Combine the chili sauce, salad oil, corn syrup, vinegar, garlic, salt and pepper and blend until smooth. Place shrimp and lemon wedges on skewers. Broil over medium coals of hibachi for 6 to 8 minutes on each side, brushing with vinegar mixture occasionally.

Mrs. Bill Wiese, Auburn, Alabama

buffet meals

Buffet service is the fun and easy way to serve a few or a crowd. You plan carefully in advance . . . cook your favorite, most praised dishes . . . and set them out on a flat surface so that your guests can serve themselves. The surface may be a table, a series of card tables, a hutch, a sideboard, or even a desk. Your guests form a line and select the portions they want from the variety you offer.

It sounds simple and, in fact, it is. But it does take careful planning on your part. Begin by making your guest list with the buffet in mind. The core of entertainment at any buffet party is conversation, so be certain to include both talkers and listeners among your guests. Decide whether you will phone or mail your invitations. And issue your invitations in plenty of time to allow your guests the fun of anticipation. Consider, too, using placecards. Unless your guests know each other well, placecards are almost a necessity — as well as a thoughtful gesture on your part.

PLANNING YOUR MENU

Once you have determined how many guests you will have, turn your attention to the menu. You'll want a menu that is within your budget yet delicious . . . featuring foods that mix and match well . . . and that can be prepared early, well before the buffet. Most of all, you'll want to feature dishes that can stand on the buffet table without losing flavor, texture, or eye appeal.

Decide on an entree, and build the remainder of your menu around it. For a seated buffet, any entree is appropriate, but if your guests are going to be eating from plates in their laps or on small trays, choose an entree which does not require cutting with a knife. A main-dish casserole . . . a chafing dish entree such as beef stroganoff . . . or a stew or meat pie are all excellent main courses for buffets. And, of course, you'll want to choose first courses, salads, and desserts which complement the flavor, texture, and color of your entree.

After you have chosen your recipes, read them carefully and list all the ingredients you will need. Check your cupboards and refrigerator to see which you have on hand, and shop for those you'll need. Unless you are buying perishables such as fresh vegetables or seafood, you'll want to do your shopping at least a day or two in advance of the buffet. Experienced hostesses recommend that you make a schedule showing what tasks you will do on each day before the party. As many foods as possible should be prepared well in advance and frozen, then thawed on the day of your buffet.

All these advance preparations will help you achieve the goal of every buffet — to relax and enjoy the event just as much as your guests.

SERVING THE BUFFET

As your guests arrive, seat them in the living room. When most are present, serve appetizers and punch or cocktails. (Here's a hint from good hostesses: be sure to have non-alcoholic drinks available if you serve cocktails.) Serving the first course in the living room keeps your guests away from the buffet and kitchen areas while the finishing touches are put on the meal. It also enables any late-arriving guests to join the group inconspicuously.

Choose appetizers that are easy to eat without a fork or plate — antipasto, bits of seafood or meat on toothpicks, and other "finger foods." A few minutes before the first course ends, excuse yourself and fill the water glasses, remove cold foods from the refrigerator, and prepare hot foods for serving. Even if you are lucky enough to have help in preparing the buffet, you will still want to look over the food before calling in your guests.

As hostess, you should be near the buffet table — you might help serve the entree or salad. While you are doing this, the host or your maid should clear the first course from the living room. If the host performs this task, he will join the buffet line when he finishes, freeing you to join your guests.

Your guests' first sight of the buffet should be impressive. On this occasion, you can prepare a spectacularly beautiful centerpiece without having to wonder about people trying to look around or over it during conversations. You can bring out your very best serving pieces, and convert other eye-pleasing pieces into servers. That silver or pewter bowl can hold sharply flavored vegetable condiments. That huge punch bowl might be just what you need to serve boubillaisse from. A buffet is the perfect occasion to bring out all those long-neglected serving pieces.

Arrange the buffet table in careful sequence. You'll want plates, entree, vegetables (if any), and salads following each other in that order. If your guests are eating away from the table, arrange silverware, napkins, and beverage glasses at the end of the table. It is preferable, if at all possible, to have people eating at tables where silver, napkins, and glasses are set up in readiness for them.

Although both entree and vegetable can fit on the plate without any problem, there may be difficulty managing the salad. In such cases, serve the salad as a separate course either before or after the entree, or plan a salad which is a self-contained unit. A great buffet salad might be half an avocado filled with crabmeat or vegetable salad. Other equally perfect salad recipes are in the pages that follow.

Rolls and relishes may be passed from guest to guest after they are seated. All buffet breads should be pre-buttered. One accompaniment which invariably sparks up a buffet is a sweet jam or jelly, especially the jewel-bright kinds.

SERVING HINTS

Whatever you choose to serve, hot foods should be very hot and cold foods icy. Casseroles can fit over candle warmers which will keep them at serving temperatures. If you have chafing dishes, by all means use them. They are lovely to look at as well as extremely functional! Cold foods can be kept at the proper temperature by setting the serving dish in a plate of crushed ice. Mix a little rock salt with the ice and it will not melt quickly, even at room temperature.

When your guests have finished with the main course, you or a guest you designate should offer them coffee and tea. Plates may be removed either by a helper, if you're fortunate enough to have one, or by you. Some hostesses ask their guests to bring their plates to a serving cart or table cleared for just that purpose.

If you have a maid, let her practice clearing the table. The correct procedure is for her to stand at the guest's left, and with her left hand, she removes the dinner plate and transfers it to her right hand. She then removes the salad plate with her left hand, transferring it to her right hand. (All this goes on behind the guest.) She moves to another guest and repeats the procedure, beginning this time with the salad plate. When she has cleared two places, she takes the plates to the kitchen and returns to clear another two.

While coffee and tea are being served, you, as the hostess, take charge of the dessert. Dessert may range from beautiful and elaborate crepes suzette or cherries jubilee to fruit plucked from the buffet centerpiece. You may want to prepare the dessert plates in the kitchen and serve them to each guest or you may present dessert as a separate course and allow guests to go through the buffet line once again. Whatever your preference, you'll want to be certain your guests have a dessert which complements the main course and which can be easily handled. Don't forget — they'll be trying to manage coffee at the same time!

BUFFET EXTRAS

Many hostesses wonder about using background music at buffet parties. As mentioned earlier, the best entertainment at buffets is conversation. Music, if present at all, should not drown out talk.

Buffets are not limited to suppers — there are breakfasts . . . brunches . . . luncheons . . . teas . . . and late evening suppers. But every buffet has certain elements in common and most important among these is the need for advance planning. Careful planning and a step-by-step schedule will enable you to relax and enjoy the party and your guests' company. And with the recipes you'll find in the pages that follow — family-proven favorites of southern homemakers — you can be certain of serving buffet-perfect foods!

145

Double Summer Salad (page 154)

buffet salads

Hot or cold . . . appetizer or meal-sized, salads bring mouth-watering variety to your buffet. They are versatile enough to complement every meal from the lightest ladies' luncheon to the most elegant party buffet.

Smart southern homemakers have long depended on salads both as main dishes and as accompaniments to their meals. And in the pages that follow you will find they have developed a wonderfully varied world of salad recipes just right for buffets — no problems with unmanageable pieces of salad, no hard-to-handle dressings! Each recipe has been developed to the peak of perfection, served to both family and friends, and then proudly submitted to be part of this Cookbook Library.

The pick of these recipes are on the pages that follow. There are fruit salad recipes — including one for an Avocado Salad Ring with Frosted Fruits that is pretty enough to double as your centerpiece. Another striking-looking salad is Chicken Salad en Cornucopia — as beautiful as it is tasty.

Accompaniment salads come in for their share of attention, too, with such unusual recipes as Crab Aspic . . . Creole Bean Salad . . . and many, many more.

Yes, to add that extra flavor note that only a salad can bring to your buffet meal, you'll depend on this section every time for home-tested, sure-to-please recipes.

AVOCADO SALAD RING WITH FROSTED FRUITS

1 pkg. lime gelatin	1 c. heavy cream, whipped
1 c. boiling water	2 c. mashed avocados
1 tbsp. lemon juice	Salad greens
3 tbsp. minced parsley	Frosted Fruits
3/4 c. mayonnaise	Lorenzo Dressing
1/2 tsp. salt	

Dissolve the gelatin in boiling water in a bowl and add the lemon juice. Chill until partially set. Fold in the parsley, mayonnaise, salt, whipped cream and avocados and pour into a large, oiled ring mold. Chill until firm. Unmold on salad greens and surround with Frosted Fruits. Serve with Lorenzo Dressing.

Frosted Fruits

1 egg white	Stemmed cherries
Sm. grape clusters	Sugar
Whole strawberries	

Beat egg white with 2 tablespoons water. Dip fruits in egg white, then roll in sugar. Place on paper towels until dry.

Lorenzo Dressing

2/3 c. olive oil	1 tsp. salt
1/3 c. vinegar	1 c. chopped watercress
1 c. chili sauce	1/4 tsp. paprika

Place all ingredients in a jar and cover. Shake well to blend.

Mrs. Walter R. Novak, Jr., Houston, Texas

BUFFET PEACH SALAD IN WINE JELLY

1 can spiced peaches	1/2 c. cold water
1 3-oz. package cream cheese	2 c. boiling water
Cream	1 c. sugar
1/2 c. chopped nuts	3 tbsp. lemon juice
2 tbsp. unflavored gelatin	1 c. sherry or port

Drain the peaches and remove seeds. Soften the cream cheese in a bowl and add enough cream to moisten. Stir in the nuts. Stuff cavities of peaches with cream cheese mixture. Soften gelatin in cold water. Add the boiling water and sugar and stir until dissolved. Add the lemon juice and sherry. Place thin layer of gelatin mixture in a mold and chill until partially set. Place the peaches in gelatin in the mold and cover with remaining gelatin mixture. Chill until firm.

Claud W. Dodd, Durant, Mississippi

STRAWBERRY GLACE

2 sm. packages strawberry gelatin	1/2 c. chopped nuts 1 pt. whole strawberries,
2 c. boiling water	sweetened
2 c. cold water	Pineapple sherbet
1 8-oz. package cream cheese	

Dissolve the gelatin in boiling water in a bowl. Stir in the cold water and chill until slightly thickened. Soften the cream cheese and shape into balls. Roll in nuts. Place alternate layers of cheese balls and strawberries in 9-inch ring mold, covering each layer with gelatin. Chill until firm. Unmold and fill center with sherbet. One large package frozen strawberries, thawed, may be substituted for fresh strawberries. 6-8 servings.

Mrs. Peter Wiese, Birmingham, Alabama

CONGEALED SALAD WITH FRESH FRUIT

3 env. unflavored gelatin	1 tsp. salt
1 1/4 c. cold water	Dash of cayenne pepper
1 2/3 c. boiling water	3 tbsp. chopped pimento
2 c. grated Cheddar cheese	3 tbsp. chopped stuffed
3/4 c. mayonnaise	olives
1 tsp. dry mustard	1 tbsp. fresh lemon juice

Soften the gelatin in cold water. Add the boiling water and stir until gelatin is dissolved. Chill until slightly thickened. Beat with an electric mixer or rotary beater until fluffy. Combine the cheese, mayonnaise, mustard, salt and cayenne pepper and mix well. Fold into the gelatin, then fold in the pimento and olives. Turn into an oiled 1-quart mold and chill until firm. Garnish with assorted fresh fruit and sprinkle fruit with lemon juice. 6-8 servings.

Congealed Salad with Fresh Fruit (above)

ORANGE-FIG RING

1 No. 303 can figs	1 3-oz. package cream
Juice of 1 lemon	cheese
Juice of 1 orange	2 tsp. Worcestershire sauce
1 3-oz. package orange	1/4 c. chopped pecans
gelatin	

Drain the figs and reserve liquid. Mix reserved liquid with lemon and orange juice and add enough water to make 1 3/4 cups liquid. Heat to boiling point. Add the gelatin and stir until dissolved. Chill until partially set. Soften the cream cheese and add Worcestershire sauce and pecans. Mix well. Cover each fig with cream cheese mixture and arrange in ring mold. Pour gelatin over figs and chill until firm. Serve on salad greens.

Mrs. Alfred J. Gipson, Decherd, Tennessee

FRUIT SALAD ANTIGUA

1/2 c. water	2 mangoes, peeled and diced
1 c. sugar	2 bananas, diced
2 tbsp. lime juice	1 ripe papaya, diced
2 oranges, peeled and diced	

Mix the water, sugar and lime juice in a saucepan and bring to a boil. Reduce heat and simmer for 5 minutes. Cool. Combine remaining ingredients in a bowl and pour syrup over fruits. Chill. Serve in fruit cups over crushed ice.

Mrs. L. B. Bannister, Raleigh, North Carolina

FRUIT SALAD WITH CHEESE

1 can crushed pineapple	4 bananas, sliced
1/2 lb. hoop cheese, grated	2 tbsp. mayonnaise
1 lge. jar maraschino cherries	

Drain the pineapple and mix with cheese in a bowl. Drain and quarter the cherries and add to pineapple mixture. Add the bananas and mayonnaise and mix well. Chill.

Mrs. Chris Eberlan, San Augustine, Texas

GOLDEN FLORIDIAN SALAD

1 lge. ripe papaya	Juice of 2 lemons
3 temple oranges	Dash of salt
1 apple	4 tbsp. sugar (opt.)
1 15-oz. can crushed pineapple	

Peel and dice the papaya, oranges and apple. Place in a bowl. Add the pineapple, lemon juice, salt and sugar and mix well. Cover and refrigerate overnight.

Mrs. Lucille Keenan, St. Petersburg, Florida

CURRIED CHICKEN-GRAPE MINGLE

3 c. diced cooked chicken
1 1/2 c. thinly sliced celery
1 c. green seedless grapes
2 tbsp. lemon juice
1 1/4 tsp. salt
1/4 tsp. pepper

1 1/2 tsp. curry powder
6 tbsp. mayonnaise
Lettuce
3 tbsp. slivered toasted
  almonds

Combine all ingredients except lettuce and almonds in a bowl and toss lightly. Chill. Serve on lettuce and garnish with almonds. 6 servings.

Lois Pullen, Baton Rouge, Louisiana

SORRENTO SALAD

3 c. diced cooked chicken
1 c. chopped celery
1/4 c. chopped red
  pepper (opt.)
1/2 tsp. salt
1/2 tsp. pepper
2/3 c. Italian bleu cheese
  dressing

1/2 c. orange sections, cut up
1/2 c. grapefruit sections,
  cut in sm. pieces
1/2 c. diced avocado
Salad greens
1 1/2 c. orange sections
1 1/2 c. grapefruit sections
1 avocado, cut in wedges

Combine the chicken, celery and red pepper in a bowl and sprinkle with salt and pepper. Add the bleu cheese dressing and mix well. Chill. Add cut orange and grapefruit sections and diced avocado and mix lightly. Turn into bowl lined with salad greens. Surround chicken salad mixture with orange and grapefruit sections and avocado wedges. Serve with additional bleu cheese dressing. Dip diced avocado and avocado wedges in orange or grapefruit juice to keep avocado from turning dark. 6 servings.

Sorrento Salad (above)

ALMOND-SESAME-CHICKEN SALAD

4 tbsp. sugar	Oil
3 tsp. salt	1 head crisp lettuce, shredded
2 tsp. monosodium glutamate	4 green onions, cut in thin
1 tsp. pepper	strips
1/2 c. salad oil	3/4 c. slivered toasted almonds
6 tbsp. white vinegar	4 tbsp. toasted sesame seed
3 boiled chicken breasts	1/2 c. fried noodles

Combine first 6 ingredients in a jar and cover. Shake well. Remove chicken from bone and shred in small pieces. Fry, small amount at a time, in deep, hot oil until crisp. Drain. Mix with lettuce and onions in a bowl. Add the dressing and toss. Top with almonds, sesame seed and noodles. 8 servings.

Mrs. John Martin, Montgomery, Alabama

CHICKEN SALAD EN CORNUCOPIA

1 10-oz. package frozen puff	1/3 c. mayonnaise
pastry shells, thawed	1 tsp. instant chicken
2 c. diced cooked chicken	bouillon
2 tbsp. lemon juice	1/4 tsp. salt
1/2 c. chopped celery	1/4 tsp. pepper
2 chopped hard-cooked eggs	3 drops of hot pepper sauce

Roll out each puff pastry shell on a floured board to a 6-inch circle and trim edge evenly. Start at outer edge and cut each circle into a continuous strip 3/4 inch wide. Wind strip over outside of an aluminum foil cone, starting at pointed end. Dampen and overlap edges of strip to seal. Place on ungreased cookie sheet. Bake at 425 degrees for 20 minutes. Cool on wire rack and remove aluminum cones. Place the chicken in a medium bowl. Add lemon juice and toss well. Add the celery and eggs. Combine the mayonnaise, instant chicken bouillon, salt, pepper and hot pepper sauce and mix until smooth. Add to chicken mixture and toss well. Chill for at least 1 hour. Fill pastry shells with chicken mixture, using about 1/2 cup for each shell. 6 servings.

Mrs. Gertrude Lacy, Tampa, Florida

JELLIED VEAL

2 tbsp. unflavored gelatin	1/2 c. diced carrots
2 c. beef bouillon	1 c. diced celery
3 c. diced veal	Tomato wedges
1 1/2 tsp. salt	Peas

Soften the gelatin in bouillon in a saucepan. Place over low heat and stir until gelatin is dissolved. Chill until thickened. Add remaining ingredients except tomato wedges and peas. Arrange tomato wedges and peas in individual molds and add gelatin mixture. Chill until firm. Serve on lettuce.

Mrs. Joe Sheldon, Rock Hill, South Carolina

JELLIED BEEF SALAD

1 env. unflavored gelatin	1 c. diced cooked beef
1 3/4 c. water	1/2 c. diced celery
2 bouillon cubes	1/2 c. cooked green peas,
1 1/2 tbsp. lemon juice	drained
1 tsp. grated onion	

Soften the gelatin in 1/2 cup water in a saucepan, then add bouillon cubes. Place over low heat and stir until gelatin and bouillon are dissolved. Remove from heat and stir in remaining water, lemon juice and onion. Chill until partially set. Fold in the beef, celery and peas. Turn into a 3-cup mold and chill until firm. Serve on lettuce. 4 servings.

Guadalupe Gonzalez, Alice, Texas

PARTY PORK CROWN

1 3-oz. package celery	1/2 tsp. prepared mustard
gelatin	1/4 tsp. salt
1 c. hot water	2 c. diced cooked pork
1/2 c. cold water	1 8-oz. can peas, drained
1 tbsp. cider vinegar	Romaine leaves
1/2 c. mayonnaise or salad dressing	

Dissolve the gelatin in hot water in a bowl and stir in cold water and vinegar. Stir in the mayonnaise, mustard and salt and chill until partially set. Beat until light. Fold in pork and peas and spoon into 4-cup ring mold. Chill until firm. Unmold onto serving plate and garnish with romaine leaves. 4-6 servings.

Mrs. Allie C. Woodcock, New Orleans, Louisiana

CRAB LOUIS SALAD

3 cans crab meat	1/2 c. chili sauce
6 c. shredded lettuce	2 tbsp. horseradish
2 hard-cooked eggs, diced	4 tsp. lemon juice
2 tbsp. chopped chives	1 tsp. salt
2 med. peeled tomatoes,	1/4 tsp. pepper
quartered	1/3 c. chopped scallions
1 1/3 c. mayonnaise	2 tbsp. chopped capers
1/3 c. heavy cream	3/4 tsp. Worcestershire sauce

Drain and flake the crab meat and place in a large salad bowl. Add the lettuce and mix well. Sprinkle with eggs and chives. Garnish with tomato wedges. Combine remaining ingredients for dressing and mix well. Pour dressing over salad and toss lightly. 5 servings.

Mrs. Albert Barnes, Tuscaloosa, Alabama

CRAB ASPIC

2 env. unflavored gelatin	1 c. chopped celery
1/2 c. cold water	1 sm. onion, chopped
1 can tomato soup	1/4 c. chopped green pepper
3 3-oz. packages cream	1 c. Thousand Island dressing
cheese	1 7 1/2-oz. can crab meat

Soften the gelatin in water. Heat the soup in a double boiler. Add the cream cheese and gelatin and stir until cheese melts. Add the celery, onion, green pepper, dressing and crab meat and place in a mold. Refrigerate for 3 hours or until firm. 8 servings.

Mrs. R. C. Scott, Hickory Flats, Mississippi

DOUBLE SUMMER SALAD

2 c. frozen orange and	1/2 c. chopped onion
grapefruit sections	1 tbsp. chopped parsley
2 3-oz. packages lemon gelatin	3 drops of hot sauce
1/2 tsp. crushed rosemary	1/3 c. mayonnaise
leaves	1 tsp. prepared mustard
2 6-oz. packages frozen	3/4 c. sliced celery
Alaska King crab	

Thaw the orange and grapefruit sections. Drain and reserve juice. Prepare the gelatin according to package directions, using reserved juice to replace part of the water. Add the rosemary and orange and grapefruit sections and mix. Pour into a 1 1/2-quart ring mold and chill until set. Thaw the King crab according to package directions and drain thoroughly. Flake the crab meat and place in a bowl. Mix with remaining ingredients and chill. Unmold the gelatin ring on a serving plate and fill center with crab mixture. Garnish base of mold with salad greens, if desired. 6 servings.

Photograph for this recipe on page 146.

LOBSTER SALAD

5 med. lobster-tails	1/2 c. mayonnaise
1 1/2 c. diced celery	1/2 c. sour cream
1 tsp. minced onion	2 lge. tomatoes, chopped
1 tsp. lemon juice	6 lettuce leaves
1 tsp. paprika	

Cook the lobster-tails in 5 quarts boiling water for about 15 minutes or until lobster-tails are light pink. Remove from water and cool. Remove lobster from shells and cut in small pieces. Blend in remaining ingredients except lettuce leaves and mix well. Serve on lettuce leaves and garnish with paprika, if desired. 6 servings.

Mrs. Charlie R. Baker, Key West, Florida

German Tuna-Potato Salad (below)

GERMAN TUNA-POTATO SALAD

2 6 1/2 to 7-oz. cans tuna	1/2 tsp. paprika
6 slices bacon, chopped	1/4 tsp. salt
1/2 c. chopped celery	1/4 tsp. celery seed
1/2 c. chopped onion	1 c. water
2 tbsp. chopped red pepper	1/2 c. vinegar
3 tbsp. sugar	3 c. sliced cooked potatoes
1 tbsp. flour	Chopped parsley to taste

Drain the tuna and break into large pieces. Fry the bacon in a 10-inch frypan until crisp and drain on absorbent paper. Cook the celery, onion and red pepper in bacon fat in the frypan until tender. Combine the sugar, flour, paprika, salt and celery seed and stir into onion mixture. Add the water and vinegar gradually and cook until thickened, stirring constantly. Combine dressing with the potatoes, bacon and tuna and mix lightly. Chill. Serve on a bed of mixed greens. 6 servings.

COLD SALMON WITH CUCUMBER DRESSING

2 med. cucumbers	2 tbsp. vinegar
1/2 c. heavy cream	Dash of hot sauce
1/4 c. mayonnaise	1 lge. can salmon, chilled
1 tsp. salt	

Grate the cucumbers and drain for 15 minutes. Whip the cream until stiff and fold in the mayonnaise, salt, vinegar, hot sauce and cucumbers. Drain the salmon and remove skin and bones. Arrange on lettuce and garnish with lemon. Serve with cucumber dressing. 6 servings.

Mrs. Milton R. Moore, Sheppard AFB, Texas

SHRIMP REMOULADE

1 1/2 c. salad oil	1 c. chopped celery
1/2 c. prepared mustard	1/4 c. chopped parsley
1/3 c. white wine vinegar	2 tbsp. chopped scallions
2 tsp. salt	1 tbsp. chopped green pepper
2 tsp. paprika	3 lb. cooked cleaned shrimp
2 tsp. hot sauce	1 lge. head lettuce, shredded
2 hard-cooked eggs, chopped	

Combine the oil, mustard, vinegar, salt, paprika and hot sauce in a bowl and beat until blended. Add the eggs, celery, parsley, scallions, green pepper and shrimp and toss well. Cover and refrigerate for 12 hours, stirring occasionally. Serve over lettuce. 8-10 servings.

Mrs. F. R. DeBray, Mobile, Alabama

CREOLE BEAN SALAD

1 No. 2 can kidney beans, drained	1/8 tsp. pepper
1/4 c. diced celery	2 strips fried bacon, crumbled
3 dill pickles, chopped	1/4 c. mayonnaise
1 sm. onion, chopped	1 tsp. prepared mustard
2 hard-boiled eggs, chopped	Dash of hot sauce
1/2 tsp. salt	2 tbsp. grated Parmesan cheese

Mix all ingredients in a bowl and chill. 6 servings.

Mrs. W. H. Stanley, Texarkana, Arkansas

POTATO ENSALADA

2 lge. potatoes	2 med. carrots, grated
1 sm. white onion, sliced into rings	1 med. green pepper, chopped
Chili Dressing	1/2 c. sliced pitted ripe olives
6 c. torn lettuce	

Cook the potatoes in boiling, salted water for 30 minutes or until tender. Drain and cool. Peel and slice thin. Place the potatoes and onion rings in separate bowls and drizzle 1/4 cup Chili Dressing over each. Chill for several hours, stirring occasionally. Line a salad bowl with lettuce. Arrange potato slices, onion slices, carrots and green peppers in bowl and place olives in center. Drizzle with remaining Chili Dressing.

Chili Dressing

1 1/2 tsp. chili powder	1/4 tsp. pepper
1 1/2 tsp. seasoned salt	1/2 c. vegetable oil
1 tsp. sugar	1/3 c. cider vinegar

Combine all ingredients in a small jar and cover. Shake well.

Mrs. Barbara Davis, Knoxville, Tennessee

TOMATO SAMBAL

6 ripe tomatoes, sliced
4 green onions, chopped
2 green chilies, peeled
   and chopped

1/4 c. salad oil
2 tbsp. lemon juice
1/2 tsp. salt
Grated coconut to taste

Arrange the tomato slices on serving platter. Mix remaining ingredients except coconut and pour over tomato slices. Sprinkle with coconut. May be served with curried dishes. 12 servings.

Pat Green, Montgomery, Alabama

SEA BREEZE SPINACH MOLD

1/4 c. cold water
1 10 1/2-oz. can beef
   broth
2 env. unflavored gelatin
1/4 tsp. salt
2 tbsp. lemon juice
1 c. salad dressing

1 med. onion, quartered
1 10-oz. package frozen
   chopped spinach, thawed
4 hard-cooked eggs, quartered
1/2 lb. cooked bacon,
   crumbled

Pour the cold water and 1/4 cup beef broth into blender container and sprinkle with gelatin. Let stand until gelatin is softened. Heat remaining beef broth in a saucepan to boiling point. Add to blender container and cover. Process at low speed until gelatin is dissolved, using a rubber spatula to push gelatin granules into the broth mixture. Add the salt, lemon juice and salad dressing and process until well blended. Add the onion and cover. Process at high speed until onion is chopped. Add the spinach and eggs and cover. Process at high speed just until eggs are coarsely chopped. Stir in the bacon and turn into a 6-cup mold. Chill until firm. Unmold and garnish with cherry tomatoes. 8 servings.

Sea Breeze Spinach Mold (above)

To give bakery breads a just-baked appearance, sprinkle with powdered sugar or top with whipped cream and strawberries. See pages 164 and 165 for special sweet breads and cakes.

buffet breads and desserts

Breads and desserts you serve at a buffet meal have to be extra-special. They must be just right for the main course . . . easily handled . . . and readily served. That's a tall order, but creative *Southern Living* homemakers have developed bread and dessert recipes just waiting for you to serve.

There are biscuits . . . hot breads . . . muffins . . . rolls . . . and many other buffet breads. There is a recipe for Cheese Biscuits that are so sharply-flavored and delicious, they don't need any butter. And that's a bonus for buffet serving! There is a recipe for unusual tasting Danish Nut Horns and another one for lively-flavored Herb Bread Sticks. And these are just a few of the many melt-in-your-mouth recipes you'll discover.

The dessert recipes are just as good — and as varied. Every kind of dessert from Petits Fours to Lemon Chess Tarts is included. Think how your guests will enjoy Mixed Fruit-Champagne Compote . . . Bisque Tortoni . . . or any one of the buffet-perfect desserts in the pages that follow.

When you are thinking of celebrating a special occasion — or transforming an ordinary meal into a happening — think buffet. And when you plan your buffet, you'll want to try these breads and desserts — for that just-right touch!

HERBED PINWHEELS

1 c. butter, softened	4 c. sifted all-purpose flour
1/4 c. chopped parsley	2 tbsp. baking powder
1/2 tsp. oregano leaves	2 tsp. salt
1/4 tsp. tarragon leaves	2/3 c. vegetable shortening
1/4 tsp. ground thyme	1 1/2 c. milk
1/8 tsp. pepper	1 egg

Whip the butter with parsley, oregano, tarragon, thyme and pepper, then let stand for 1 hour to blend flavors. Mix the flour, baking powder and salt in a bowl and cut in shortening until mixture looks like coarse meal. Stir in the milk. Knead about 10 times on a floured board and divide the dough in half. Roll out each half into a 12 x 10-inch rectangle. Spread half the herb mixture on each rectangle, then roll up each rectangle from 12-inch side and seal edge. Cut each roll into 24 1/2-inch pinwheels and place pinwheels in ungreased muffin pans. Beat the egg with 2 tablespoons water and brush over pinwheels. Bake in a 425-degree oven for 10 to 15 minutes or until golden brown.

Photograph for this recipe on page 145.

CHEESE BISCUITS

2 c. sifted flour	1/4 c. shortening
3 tsp. baking powder	1/3 c. grated sharp cheese
1 tsp. salt	3/4 c. milk

Mix the flour, baking powder and salt in a bowl and cut in shortening until mixture resembles coarse cornmeal. Stir in the cheese. Add the milk and stir just

Cranberry-Pumpkin Muffins (page 161)

until mixed. Roll out on a floured surface and cut with biscuit cutter. Place on ungreased cookie sheet. Bake at 425 degrees for 12 to 15 minutes or until browned.

Mrs. Morris E. Cavenaugh, Magnolia, North Carolina

CARROT MUFFINS

1 c. shortening	1 1/2 c. grated carrots
1/2 c. (packed) brown sugar	1 1/2 c. flour
1 egg, beaten	1/2 tsp. salt
1/4 tsp. nutmeg	1 tsp. baking powder
1/2 tsp. cinnamon	

Cream the shortening and sugar in a bowl. Add egg and mix well. Dissolve the spices in 1 tablespoon hot water and add to sugar mixture. Add the carrots and mix. Sift dry ingredients together. Add to carrot mixture and mix well. Spoon into greased muffin cups. Bake at 375 degrees for about 25 minutes. 12 muffins.

Mrs. Louise Emerson, Nashville, Tennessee

DELICIOUS BRAN MUFFINS

1/3 c. butter	1 1/4 c. bran
1/2 c. sugar	Dash of salt
1 lge. egg, beaten	1/2 tsp. nutmeg
1 c. sour cream	1 tsp. soda
1/2 c. seedless raisins	2 c. flour
2 tbsp. molasses	1/2 c. chopped walnuts

Cream the butter in a bowl. Add the sugar and egg and beat well. Add the sour cream, raisins, molasses and bran and mix well. Sift the salt, nutmeg, soda and flour together and add the walnuts. Add to sour cream mixture and mix well. Fill well-greased muffin tins 2/3 full. Bake at 375 degrees for 20 minutes. 16 muffins.

Mrs. Elsie Gray, Morgantown, West Virginia

CRANBERRY-PUMPKIN MUFFINS

2 1/4 c. sifted all-purpose flour	1/3 c. oil
1 tbsp. baking powder	2 eggs
1 tsp. salt	3/4 c. canned pumpkin
3/4 c. sugar	1 1/2 c. coarsely chopped fresh cranberries
1/2 tsp. allspice	

Preheat oven to 400 degrees. Sift the flour, baking powder, salt, sugar and allspice together into a bowl. Mix the oil, eggs and pumpkin until blended and add all at once to the sifted ingredients. Stir until just blended and fold in the cranberries. Spoon into greased muffin cups. Bake for 20 to 25 minutes or until muffins are lightly browned. Let stand for 5 minutes. Remove from pan and serve warm or cool. 12 muffins.

Bohemian Fruit Buns (below)

BOHEMIAN FRUIT BUNS

3 to 4 c. unsifted flour	1 egg, at room temperature
1/4 c. sugar	Peanut oil
1 tsp. salt	2 c. canned fruit pie
1 pkg. dry yeast	filling
3/4 c. milk	Confectioners' sugar
1/4 c. water	Whipped cream
1/4 c. margarine	

Mix 1 cup flour, sugar, salt and yeast thoroughly in a large bowl. Combine the milk, water and margarine in a saucepan and place over low heat until the liquids are warm. Margarine does not need to melt. Add to sugar mixture gradually and beat for 2 minutes with electric mixer at medium speed, scraping bowl occasionally. Add the egg and 1/2 cup flour and beat at high speed for 2 minutes, scraping bowl occasionally. Stir in enough remaining flour to make a soft dough. Turn out onto lightly floured board and knead for 8 to 10 minutes or until smooth and elastic. Place in a greased bowl, turning to grease top, and cover. Let rise in warm place, free from draft, for about 1 hour or until doubled in bulk. Punch down and turn out onto lightly floured board. Roll out to 1/2-inch thickness and cut with a 3-inch biscuit cutter. Place on greased baking sheets. Cover and let rise in warm place, free from draft, for about 1 hour or until doubled in bulk. Handle buns as little as possible to prevent falling. Fry in deep oil at 375 degrees for 2 to 3 minutes or until brown on both sides. Drain on paper towels and cool. Make a hole in center of each bun and fill with about 1 1/2 tablespoons fruit pie filling. Sprinkle with confectioners' sugar or top with whipped cream and serve. 18 buns.

DANISH NUT HORNS

Sugar	1/4 tsp. salt
4 c. flour	2 c. shortening

4 eggs, beaten
1 pkg. yeast
1/2 c. evaporated milk

1 c. ground walnuts
2 tbsp. honey

Place 1 tablespoon sugar, flour and salt in large bowl and cut in shortening as for pie crust. Add the eggs and mix. Dissolve the yeast in 1/4 cup warm milk and add to flour mixture. Blend well. Cover with waxed paper and refrigerate overnight. Divide dough in 4 parts. Roll out each part to a circle on board sprinkled with sugar and cut in pie-shaped wedges. Combine the walnuts, honey, remaining milk and 1/4 cup sugar. Place 1 teaspoon walnut mixture at wide end of each wedge and roll from wide end to point. Place on cookie sheet, point side down, and shape in crescent. Bake at 350 degrees for 20 minutes. Strawberry or apricot preserves or peanut butter may be substituted for walnut filling, if desired.

Stella Bartsch, Glendale, West Virginia

HERB BREADSTICKS

1/2 c. scalded milk
1/4 c. shortening
1 tbsp. sugar
1 1/2 tsp. salt
1/2 c. water
1 pkg. yeast

1 egg, beaten
1/2 tsp. nutmeg
1 tsp. leaf sage
2 tsp. caraway seed
3 c. sifted flour

Combine the milk, shortening, sugar and salt in a bowl and mix well. Add the water and cool to lukewarm. Add the yeast and stir until yeast is dissolved. Blend in the egg, nutmeg, sage and caraway seed. Add flour gradually and mix until blended. Place in a greased bowl and cover. Refrigerate for at least 2 hours. Divide into 36 parts and roll each part into 8-inch cylindrical strip. Place on a greased baking sheet 1 inch apart and let rise until doubled in bulk. Bake at 400 degrees for 15 minutes.

Margaret Davis, Belton, Texas

SWEDISH BREAD

2 c. milk
3/4 c. molasses
Sugar
2 tbsp. shortening

2 tsp. salt
2 pkg. yeast
5 lb. (about) flour

Mix the milk, 2 cups water, molasses, 1/2 cup sugar, shortening and salt in a saucepan and bring to a boil. Cool until lukewarm. Mix the yeast, 1/4 cup water and 1 teaspoon sugar in a bowl and stir until dissolved. Add the milk mixture and mix well. Mix in enough flour to make a stiff dough and let rise until doubled in bulk. Punch down, then knead on a floured surface until smooth. Place in well-greased loaf pans and let rise until doubled in bulk. Bake at 350 degrees for 40 to 50 minutes.

Mrs. Ben T. Jacob, Georgetown, Texas

HOLIDAY CAKE

3/4 c. butter or margarine	1 tsp. baking powder
3/4 c. sugar	3/8 c. cream
2 eggs	1/4 c. water
1/4 c. ground almonds	Bread crumbs
1 tsp. vanilla	Whipped cream
1 1/2 c. flour	Strawberries

Cream the butter and sugar in a bowl. Add the eggs, one at a time, beating well after each addition. Stir in the almonds and vanilla. Sift the flour with baking powder. Mix the cream and milk and add to creamed mixture alternately with flour mixture. Sprinkle a greased tube pan with bread crumbs and pour the cake batter into tube pan. Bake at 325 to 350 degrees for about 45 minutes or until cake tests done. Cool for 10 minutes, then remove from pan. Cool on a rack. Cut the cake in half crosswise and spread whipped cream on each layer. Place layers together and garnish with whole and halved strawberries.

Photograph for this recipe on page 158.

BOURBON-RAISIN CAKE

1 1/2 c. seedless raisins	1/2 tsp. cloves
2 c. boiling water	1/2 tsp. nutmeg
1/2 c. shortening	1/4 tsp. allspice
3/4 c. sugar	1/2 tsp. salt
1 egg	1 c. chopped walnuts
1 1/2 c. sifted flour	1 tbsp. bourbon
1 tsp. soda	

Place the raisins in water in a saucepan and simmer for 20 minutes. Drain and reserve 3/4 cup liquid. Cream the shortening and sugar in a bowl, then beat in egg. Sift the flour with soda, spices and salt and add to creamed mixture alternately with reserved liquid. Stir in the raisins, walnuts and bourbon and pour into 2 greased 9-inch round cake pans. Bake at 350 degrees for 25 minutes. Cool for 10 minutes and remove from pans. Cool on wire rack.

Bourbon Hard Sauce

1/4 c. butter	1 egg, beaten
3 c. sifted powdered sugar	1 tbsp. bourbon

Mix the butter with powdered sugar, egg and bourbon in a bowl and frost cake.

Mrs. F. S. Millham, Fullerton, Pennsylvania

BROWN SUGAR POUND CAKE

2 sticks margarine	3 c. cake flour
1/2 c. shortening	5 eggs
1 1-lb. box dark brown	1 c. milk
sugar	1 tsp. vanilla
1/2 tsp. baking powder	

Cream the margarine, shortening and sugar in a large bowl. Sift the baking powder and flour together. Add the eggs to creamed mixture, one at a time, beating well after each addition. Add the flour mixture alternately with milk. Add vanilla and mix well. Pour into a well-greased loaf or 10-inch tube pan. Bake at 275 degrees for 30 minutes. Increase temperature to 325 degrees and bake for 45 minutes longer or until done.

Photograph for this recipe on page 158.

BLUEBERRY HOLIDAY RING

4 c. biscuit mix	1/4 c. sugar
1 1/3 c. milk	1/2 tsp. cinnamon
1 can blueberries	1 tsp. grated orange rind
1/2 c. butter	Dash of angostura aromatic
3/4 c. dry bread crumbs	bitters
1/2 c. coarsely chopped	1 c. confectioners' sugar
walnuts or pecans	2 tbsp. orange juice

Combine the biscuit mix with milk in a bowl and prepare dough according to package directions for rolled biscuits. Knead several times on lightly floured board and roll out in a 10 x 14-inch rectangle. Drain the blueberries well. Melt the butter in a small saucepan. Stir in the bread crumbs, walnuts, sugar, cinnamon, orange rind and bitters and saute until crumbs are lightly browned. Stir in the blueberries and spread evenly over rolled out dough. Roll as for jelly roll, starting at wide end. Shape into a ring, joining ends, and place in well-greased 6-quart ring mold. Bake at 375 degrees for 30 to 35 minutes or until golden brown. Turn out of mold onto serving plate while still hot. Combine the confectioners' sugar and orange juice and stir until smooth. Spread over top of warm ring to glaze. Garnish with maraschino cherry stars and whole blueberries, if desired. Serve warm. 8-10 servings.

Blueberry Holiday Ring (above)

PETITS FOURS

1/4 c. butter	1/4 tsp. salt
1/4 c. shortening	3 tsp. baking powder
1 1/4 c. sugar	3/4 c. milk
1/2 tsp. vanilla	3/4 c. egg whites
1/4 tsp. almond extract	1/4 c. sugar
2 c. cake flour	Confectioners' sugar frosting

Cream the butter, shortening and 1 cup sugar in a large bowl. Stir in the vanilla and almond extracts. Sift dry ingredients together and add to creamed mixture alternately with milk. Beat until smooth. Beat the egg whites until soft peaks form. Add remaining sugar gradually and beat until stiff peaks form. Fold into flour mixture. Place in 2 waxed paper-lined 9 x 12-inch baking pans. Bake in 350-degree oven for 40 minutes. Cool for 10 minutes and remove from pans. Remove waxed paper and cool. Cut in squares, ovals and triangles and frost with confectioners' sugar frosting.

Charlsie Biggs, McCalla, Alabama

MIXED FRUIT-CHAMPAGNE COMPOTE

3/4 c. sugar	2 peeled peaches, quartered
2 c. water	2 peeled nectarines or
Dash of salt	apricots, quartered
1 tbsp. lemon juice	1 c. fresh pineapple wedges
2 peeled pears, quartered	1 c. dry champagne

Combine first 4 ingredients in a saucepan and bring to boiling point. Reduce heat and simmer for 5 minutes. Add the pears and cover. Simmer for 10 minutes. Add remaining fruits and cover. Simmer for 5 to 10 minutes or until fruits are tender. Cool in the syrup, then chill. Pour into a large serving bowl. Add the champagne and mix. Place bowl over crushed ice. Garnish fruit mixture with maraschino cherries. 8 servings.

Mrs. Jean McCall, Jackson, Mississippi

FRESH PEACH-RASPBERRY MOLD

12 ladyfingers, split	1 lge. egg
1 env. unflavored gelatin	1/8 tsp. salt
1/4 c. cold water	3/4 c. milk
1 c. crushed fresh peaches	1 1/2 c. heavy cream
2 tsp. lemon juice	1 tsp. vanilla
3/4 c. sugar	1 tbsp. confectioners' sugar
2 lge. egg yolks	Sweetened raspberries

Line bottom and sides of a lightly greased mold with ladyfingers. Soften the gelatin in water. Combine the peaches, lemon juice and 1/4 cup sugar. Beat the egg yolks and egg in top of a double boiler. Add remaining sugar, salt and milk and mix well. Cook over hot water until mixture coats a spoon and strain through a fine sieve into a bowl. Stir in the gelatin until dissolved. Chill until thickened. Whip 1 cup cream until stiff and fold in the custard and peach mixture. Add vanilla and pour into the prepared mold. Refrigerate until firm. Unmold onto a serving dish. Whip remaining cream with confectioners' sugar until stiff and pipe through a pastry bag with a star tube onto mold. Serve with raspberries. 6 servings.

Mrs. Carl Dix, Little Rock, Arkansas

PINEAPPLE-BANANA CHARLOTTE

Ladyfingers
1 3-oz. package lemon
  gelatin
3 tbsp. sugar
1 c. boiling water

1 8 or 9-oz. can crushed pineapple
Lemon juice
1/2 c. instant nonfat dry
  milk
2 med. bananas

Arrange ladyfingers on bottom and side of a springform pan. Mix the gelatin and sugar in a bowl. Add the boiling water and stir until dissolved. Drain the pineapple and reserve juice. Mix reserved juice, 2 tablespoons lemon juice and enough water to make 1 cup liquid and stir into gelatin. Chill until partially set. Sprinkle dry milk on gelatin mixture and beat with electric mixer at high speed until fluffy. Fold in the pineapple. Slice 1 banana and place over ladyfingers in bottom of pan. Pour in gelatin mixture. Slice remaining banana and dip slices in lemon juice. Place on top of gelatin mixture. Chill until firm.

Pineapple-Banana Charlotte (above)

167

BLONDE BROWNIES

1 c. flour	1 c. (packed) brown sugar
1/2 tsp. baking powder	1 egg, beaten
1/8 tsp. salt	1 tsp. vanilla
1/8 tsp. soda	1 6-oz. package chocolate
1/2 c. chopped nuts	chips
1/3 c. melted butter	

Sift dry ingredients together. Add the nuts and mix. Mix the butter, brown sugar, egg and vanilla in a bowl. Add the flour mixture and mix well. Place in an 8-inch square pan and sprinkle chocolate chips over top. Bake at 350 degrees for 25 minutes.

Mrs. Paul W. Frazier, Grenada, Mississippi

CREME BRULEE

1 c. sugar	1/2 tsp. salt
1 tbsp. water	1 tsp. vanilla
2 c. light cream	1/4 c. (packed) light brown
4 lge. eggs, lightly beaten	sugar

Melt 1/2 cup sugar in a small saucepan over low heat, stirring constantly to prevent burning. Add the water and cook, stirring, until smooth. Pour into a 10 x 6 x 1 1/2-inch baking dish, coating bottom of the dish completely. Cool. Heat the cream in top of a double boiler over hot water until bubbles form around edge. Combine remaining sugar, eggs, salt, and vanilla in a mixing bowl and beat in the cream gradually. Strain into prepared baking dish and place the dish in a pan of hot water. Bake at 325 degrees for 40 minutes or until a knife inserted in center comes out clean. Remove dish from the water and cool. Refrigerate until chilled. Sift the brown sugar uniformly over the top and broil 4 inches from heat for 3 to 4 minutes or until glazed, watching carefully to prevent burning. Cool. Refrigerate until chilled. 6 servings.

Mrs. Connie Bozeman, Rome, Georgia

BISQUE TORTONI

3/4 c. sugar	3 egg yolks, beaten
3/4 c. strong coffee	25 coconut macaroons
1 tbsp. butter	1 pt. whipping cream

Mix the sugar and coffee in a saucepan and bring to a boil. Cook until mixture spins a thread. Add the butter and cool. Beat in egg yolks and freeze, stirring once or twice. Roll macaroons into crumbs and line a refrigerator pan with crumbs, reserving 3/4 cup for topping. Whip the cream until stiff, adding frozen mixture slowly. Pour into prepared pan and top with reserved crumbs. Freeze. Cut in squares.

Helen Sergent, Gate City, Virginia

COFFEE-CHOCOLATE CREAM

1 9 x 5 x 1-in. layer sponge cake	2 tbsp. sugar
1/4 c. rum-flavored sugar syrup	1 1/2 tsp. instant coffee
1 pt. chocolate ice cream, softened	1 tsp. vanilla
3 tbsp. rum	1 c. heavy cream
1 pt. coffee ice cream, softened	Shaved sweetened chocolate

Line a 9 x 5 x 3-inch loaf pan with aluminum foil, having foil extend 3 inches above top of the pan. Place cake in the pan and sprinkle with rum-flavored syrup. Freeze for 1 hour. Combine the chocolate ice cream and rum and spread over cake. Freeze until firm. Spread coffee ice cream over chocolate layer and freeze until firm. Remove mold from the pan with the foil and place on a serving tray. Remove foil. Add the sugar, instant coffee and vanilla to the cream and whip until mixture forms stiff peaks. Spread over top and sides of mold. Place remaining whipped cream into a pastry bag fitted with rosette nozzle and pipe crosswise rows over top of mold. Garnish with shaved chocolate. Cut in 1-inch slices to serve. 9 servings.

Mrs. Maynard Ivy, Birmingham, Alabama

STRAWBERRY CREAM IN SWISS MERINGUES

2 c. sliced strawberries	1/8 tsp. salt
1/2 c. sifted confectioners' sugar	2 c. heavy cream
	2 tsp. vanilla

Combine the strawberries, 1/4 cup sugar and salt. Whip the cream until almost stiff. Beat in remaining sugar gradually, then add the vanilla. Fold in the strawberries and chill.

Swiss Meringues

1/4 tsp. salt	1 c. fine sugar
1/4 tsp. cream of tartar	1/2 tsp. vanilla
4 lge. egg whites	Cornstarch

Add salt and cream of tartar to the egg whites in a bowl and beat with electric mixer at high speed until soft peaks form. Beat in the sugar at low speed, 2 tablespoons at a time, then beat at high speed until stiff peaks form. Add vanilla. Draw twelve 3-inch circles on a piece of brown paper. Grease the paper lightly and dust with cornstarch. Spread each circle with a layer of meringue 1/4 inch thick. Build a border with more meringue to a height of 1 1/2 inches, leaving center unfilled. Place the paper on a cookie sheet. Bake at 250 degrees for 1 hour and 15 minutes. Turn off heat and leave meringues in the oven for 30 minutes. Remove from oven and cool. Fill meringues with strawberry mixture. 12 servings.

Mrs. Celeste Berry, Austin, Texas

Raisin-Coconut Torte (below)

RAISIN-COCONUT TORTE

1 c. peanut butter	4 eggs, beaten
2/3 c. mixed shortening and	1 1/2 c. seedless raisins
butter	1 c. flaked coconut
1 1/2 c. (packed) brown	2 c. sifted flour
sugar	2 tsp. baking powder
1 1/2 c. sugar	1 1/2 tsp. salt
1 tsp. vanilla	Whipped cream

Mix the peanut butter and shortening mixture in a bowl. Beat in sugars gradually and add vanilla. Add the eggs and mix well. Stir in raisins and coconut. Sift the flour with baking powder and salt into raisin mixture and stir well. Spread evenly in greased and floured 8-inch layer pans. Bake at 350 degrees for 30 to 35 minutes or until cakes test done. Remove from pans and cool on rack. Stack layers with whipped cream between layers.

SOUR CREAM TORTE

3 c. sifted all-purpose flour	2 c. chopped walnuts or pecans
3/4 c. sugar	2 c. sour cream
1 c. butter or margarine	1 1/2 c. confectioners' sugar
1 egg	1 tsp. vanilla

Preheat oven to 350 degrees. Mix the flour and sugar in a mixing bowl. Cut in the butter with a pastry blender or 2 knives until mixture is consistency of meal. Stir in the egg and mix well. Divide into 7 equal parts and roll each part on lightly floured surface into a 9-inch circle. Place on a baking sheet. Bake for 10 to 12 minutes or until the edges are lightly brown. Cool, then remove from baking sheet with a spatula. Mix the walnuts, sour cream, confectioners' sugar and vanilla and spread on each baked circle. Place circles on top of each other and sprinkle top with additional confectioners' sugar. Refrigerate for at least 5 hours. Cut in wedges to serve.

Mrs. Dennis P. Landry, Crowley, Louisiana

CARAMEL PECAN PIE

1/4 c. butter	3 tbsp. flour
2 c. sugar	2 tsp. vanilla
3/4 c. water	1 c. chopped pecans
4 egg yolks, beaten	2 baked pie shells
1 c. cream	1 recipe meringue

Mix the butter, sugar and water in a saucepan and cook until consistency of thick sauce. Cool. Mix the egg yolks, cream and flour and stir into the sugar mixture. Cook, stirring until thick. Remove from heat and add vanilla and pecans. Pour into pie shells and top with meringue. Bake at 350 degrees until brown. Cool.

Mrs. Ray Martin, Llano, Texas

CHOCOLATE CHIP-ALMOND PIE

6 sm. chocolate-almond bars	1/2 c. chocolate chips
17 marshmallows	1/2 c. slivered almonds
1/2 c. milk	1 baked graham cracker crust
1 c. whipping cream, whipped	

Melt the chocolate bars and marshmallows in milk in a double boiler over medium heat. Remove from water and cool. Fold in the whipped cream, chocolate chips and slivered almonds and pour into graham cracker crust. Refrigerate for at least 4 hours.

Mrs. J. C. Fryday, La Porte, Texas

PERFECT LEMON PIE

6 eggs, separated	Grated rind of 1 lemon
1 1/4 c. sugar	1 tbsp. butter
Juice of 2 lemons	1 baked pie crust

Beat the egg yolks in top of a double boiler until light. Add 1 cup sugar, lemon juice, grated rind and butter and mix well. Cook over boiling water until very thick, stirring frequently. Fold in 4 beaten egg whites and cook for 2 minutes longer. Place in pie crust. Beat remaining egg whites until stiff, adding remaining sugar gradually, and spread on pie. Bake in 325-degree oven until brown.

Eleanor B. Hyatt, Knoxville, Tennessee

STRAWBERRY MOCHA CREAM TARTLETS

4 c. sifted all-purpose flour	1/2 c. strong coffee
2 tsp. salt	1/2 c. sugar
1 1/2 c. vegetable shortening	6 egg yolks
2 pt. fresh strawberries	1 tbsp. instant coffee powder
Light corn syrup	2 tbsp. cocoa
	1 c. softened sweet butter

Combine the flour and salt in bowl. Cut in the shortening until uniform but coarse. Sprinkle with 1/2 cup water and toss with fork, then press into a ball. Roll out 1/2 of the dough at a time on a lightly floured surface to a 1/8-inch thickness. Cut into 3-inch circles, then fit inside 2 1/4-inch tart pans and prick with fork. Place on a baking sheet. Bake in a 425-degree oven for 10 minutes or until lightly browned. Cool and remove from tart pans. Brush the strawberries with corn syrup and let dry on racks. Combine the coffee and sugar and boil to the thread stage or until candy thermometer registers 234 degrees. Beat the egg yolks with the instant coffee powder and cocoa until fluffy and thick. Add the hot syrup gradually to yolks, pouring in a thin steady stream and beating constantly. Continue beating until light in color and cold, then beat in butter. Chill slightly if necessary. Pipe a ring of the butter mixture around the inside edge of each cooled tartlet shell. Place a strawberry in each shell and chill until served. 50 servings.

Photograph for this recipe on page 145.

LEMON CHESS TARTS

1/2 c. soft butter	1/3 c. lemon juice
1 1/2 c. sugar	Grated rind of 1 lemon
1 tbsp. white cornmeal	6 unbaked tart shells
4 eggs	

Cream the butter and sugar in a bowl until light and fluffy, then stir in the cornmeal. Beat in the eggs, one at a time. Add the lemon juice and grated rind and mix well. Place in tart shells. Bake at 350 degrees for 25 to 30 minutes.

Mrs. Louis A. Combs, Ooltewah, Tennessee

DATE TARTS

1 c. butter	2 eggs
1 3-oz. package cream cheese	1 c. chopped nuts
1 1/2 c. flour	1 c. chopped dates
1 c. sugar	Sifted confectioners' sugar

Cream half the butter and cream cheese in a bowl. Add the flour and mix thoroughly. Roll out on a floured board and cut with a large biscuit cutter. Place in muffin tins. Cream remaining butter and sugar in a bowl, then add eggs, one at a time, beating well after each addition. Add the nuts and dates and mix thoroughly. Place in tart shells. Bake in 350-degree oven for 15 to 20 minutes. Remove from pans carefully and sprinkle hot tarts with confectioners' sugar. Raisins or chopped candied fruits may be substituted for dates. 20 tarts.

Mrs. E. P. Gibson, Laurel Hill, North Carolina

BLUEBERRY-CREAM CHEESE PASTRIES

1 c. butter or margarine
2 c. all-purpose flour
1 c. sour cream
3 eggs, well beaten
1 tbsp. sugar
2 tbsp. melted butter or
  margarine

1 tsp. vanilla
1/2 tsp. almond extract
2 8-oz. packages cream
  cheese, softened
1 1-lb. 6-oz. can blueberry
  pie filling

Preheat oven to 375 degrees. Cut the butter into flour in a bowl until particles are very fine. Add 3 tablespoons sour cream and stir until dough leaves side of bowl. Knead on a lightly floured board several times. Divide dough into 12 pieces and press with floured fingers into bottom and side of twelve 3-inch tart or muffin tins. Beat remaining sour cream with eggs, sugar, melted butter, vanilla, almond extract and cream cheese in a bowl until smooth. Fill tarts to within 1/2 inch of the top. Any leftover cheese mixture may be baked in custard cups as a pudding and topped with blueberries. Bake tarts for 20 minutes or until light brown, then cool in pans. Unmold and spoon blueberry pie filling over top of each tart. Garnish with sweetened whipped cream.

Blueberry-Cream Cheese Pastries (above)

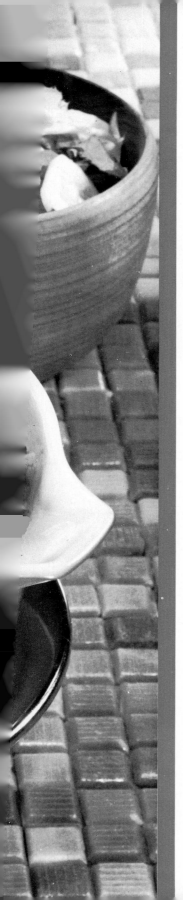

Easy Ripe Olive Jambalaya (page 182)

buffet casseroles

Ask any southern hostess from Maryland to Florida what she serves at her most successful buffet parties, and she'll probably tell you a casserole.

These popular hostesses know that for easy preparation . . . trouble-free serving . . . and oh-so-good flavor, a party-perfect casserole is just about unbeatable. From the kitchens of *Southern Living* homemakers have come recipes for their all-time favorite buffet casseroles — the dishes they serve their friends and family when nothing but the very best will do.

In the pages that follow, you'll discover the pick of these recipes — such as Beef Parmigiana, a lively blend of two favorite foods . . . Crab Biloxi, named for a popular Mississippi resort . . . and elegant Louisiana Seafood Casserole. There is a recipe for piquantly-flavored Green Peppers-Chicken au Gratin. And a typically southern food takes on South Pacific flavor in Polynesian Rice. For a great taste treat, try serving Dilled Green Beans — a wonderful way to prepare a much-loved vegetable!

These are just some of the finest home-tested recipes from southern homemakers, women famed for generations for their careful way of preparing extra-delicious foods. Serve any one of these dishes at your next buffet — then sit back and listen to the compliments flow!

175

Beef-Peach Pie (below)

BEEF-PEACH PIE

1   1-lb. 13-oz. can cling
    peach halves
1 1/2 lb. ground lean beef
1 1/2 c. soft bread crumbs
1/2 c. finely chopped onion

1 1/4 tsp. salt
2 eggs
1   8-oz. can tomato sauce
    with mushrooms

Drain the peaches and reserve 1/4 cup syrup. Mix the ground beef, crumbs, onion, salt, eggs, reserved peach syrup and 1/2 cup tomato sauce in a bowl, then turn into 8-inch round baking dish or 9-inch pie plate. Do not pack. Make depressions in beef mixture around edge of dish with back of a spoon and place peach halves, cup sides up, in depressions. Cover. Bake in 350-degree oven for about 1 hour. Remove cover. Spoon remaining tomato sauce into peach cups and over surface of beef mixture and bake for 15 to 20 minutes longer. Cut into pie-shaped wedges to serve. 6-7 servings.

BEEF PARMIGIANA

1 lge. round steak
2 eggs, beaten
2/3 c. grated Parmesan cheese
2/3 c. fine dry bread crumbs
Oil
1 onion, chopped
1/4 tsp. salt

1/4 tsp. pepper
1 tsp. sugar
1 tsp. marjoram
2 cans tomato paste
4 c. hot water
1 sm. package grated mozzarella
    cheese

Cut the steak in serving pieces and pound with a mallet. Dip in eggs. Mix the Parmesan cheese and bread crumbs and roll the steak in crumb mixture. Brown in small amount of oil in a skillet, then place in a shallow baking pan. Saute the onion in oil remaining in the skillet until tender. Add the salt, pepper, sugar, marjoram, tomato paste and water and bring to a boil. Pour half the sauce over steak and sprinkle with mozzarella cheese. Add remaining sauce. Bake for 1 hour at 350 degrees. 6 servings.

Mrs. Duane Webb, Tempe, Arizona

BEEF SOUFFLE

6 tbsp. margarine	3 c. chopped cooked beef
1/2 c. flour	2 tbsp. chopped parsley
3 c. milk	Salt and pepper to taste
1/2 c. bread crumbs	4 eggs, separated

Melt the margarine in a saucepan and stir in the flour. Add the milk and cook, stirring constantly, until thickened. Add the bread crumbs, beef, parsley, salt, pepper and beaten egg yolks and mix well. Fold in stiffly beaten egg whites. Place in a greased baking dish and place the baking dish in pan of warm water. Bake at 325 degrees for 1 hour and 30 minutes or until firm. Gravy or tomato sauce may be served with souffle. 6 servings.

Mrs. E. B. Young, Pulaski, Tennessee

SHEPHERD'S PIE

4 c. cubed cooked beef	Salt and pepper to taste
2 to 3 c. cooked vegetables	3 c. hot mashed potatoes
2 1/2 c. gravy	1 egg, well beaten

Place the beef, vegetables and gravy in a saucepan and heat to boiling point. Sprinkle with salt and pepper and pour into a 2-quart casserole. Mix the potatoes and egg well and place around edge of casserole. Bake at 425 degrees for 15 to 20 minutes or until potatoes are brown. Lamb or veal may be substituted for beef. 6-8 servings.

Mrs. A. J. Urban, Cameron, Texas

SPANISH CASSEROLE

2/3 c. rice	1/4 tsp. paprika
2 tbsp. butter or margarine	1 c. chopped celery
1 med. onion, chopped	1/4 c. chopped green peppers
1 lb. round steak, cut in cubes	1 can tomato soup
3/4 tsp. salt	

Cook the rice according to package directions. Melt the butter in a skillet. Add the onion, steak, salt and paprika and cook until steak is brown. Place 1/3 of the rice in a greased baking dish and cover with half the steak mixture. Sprinkle half the celery and green peppers over steak and cover with half the remaining rice. Place remaining steak mixture over rice and sprinkle with remaining celery and green peppers. Cover with remaining rice and pour the soup over rice. Cover. Bake at 350 degrees for 30 minutes. 6 servings.

Susan Owens, Clinton, Tennessee

VEAL CHOPS EN CASSEROLE

6 veal chops	4 c. thinly sliced potatoes
1 tsp. salt	1/3 c. finely chopped onions
Pepper to taste	1 can cream of mushroom soup
2 tbsp. butter or margarine	1 1/4 c. milk

Season the veal chops with salt and pepper. Melt the butter in a skillet. Add the chops and brown lightly on both sides. Place the potatoes in a greased 2-quart baking dish and arrange chops on potatoes. Cook the onions in butter remaining in the skillet until tender. Add the soup and milk and blend until smooth. Pour over the chops and cover. Bake at 350 degrees for 30 minutes. Uncover and bake for 30 to 40 minutes longer or until potatoes are done. 6 servings.

Mrs. Ralph Chappell, Elkin, North Carolina

VEAL AND RICE CASSEROLE

4 slices salt pork, diced	1 c. cooked rice
1 lge. onion, chopped	1 can tomato soup
4 c. diced cooked veal	2 hard-boiled eggs, sliced
Salt and pepper to taste	2 tbsp. butter or margarine
1 c. water	

Fry the salt pork and onion in a skillet for 10 minutes or until lightly browned. Add the veal, salt, pepper and water and heat thoroughly. Pour into a well-greased baking dish. Mix the rice and tomato soup and place over veal mixture. Add the eggs and dot with butter. Cover. Bake at 350 degrees for 30 minutes, adding water, if needed. 6 servings.

Opal Stout, Piedmont, Oklahoma

SWEET POTATO-PORK BUFFET

6 pork chops	1 med. onion, chopped
1 tsp. salt	1 c. water
1/8 tsp. pepper	1 tsp. Worcestershire sauce
4 med. sweet potatoes, sliced	

Brown the pork chops in small amount of fat in a skillet, then place in a large casserole. Sprinkle with half the salt and pepper. Place the sweet potatoes over chops and sprinkle with remaining salt and pepper. Saute the onion in fat remaining in the skillet until tender and add the water and Worcestershire sauce. Pour over the potatoes and cover. Bake at 375 degrees for 1 hour and 30 minutes. 6 servings.

Martha Wood, Grenada, Mississippi

PAULA RICE

1 lb. bulk sausage	1 bell pepper, chopped
3 med. onions, chopped	2 c. chopped celery

1 pkg. slivered almonds
2 pkg. chicken soup mix

1/2 c. rice
5 c. boiling water

Brown the sausage, onions, bell pepper and celery in a skillet and drain off the fat. Add remaining ingredients and mix well. Simmer for 7 minutes, then place in a 2-quart baking dish. Bake at 325 degrees for 1 hour. 6 servings.

Patsy Strickland, Waycross, Georgia

APPLE-HAM CASSEROLE

3 peeled apples, diced
2 c. chopped cooked ham
3/4 c. brown sugar
1/3 c. melted butter or margarine

1/3 c. orange juice
1 tbsp. grated orange peel
1/4 c. chopped walnuts

Combine all ingredients except the walnuts and place in a casserole. Bake at 375 degrees for 40 minutes, stirring occasionally. Top with walnuts and bake for 5 minutes longer. 5 servings.

Bessie Mae Ricks, Booneville, Mississippi

BAKED DEVILED EGGS AND HAM

10 hard-cooked eggs
1/4 c. minced parsley
1 tbsp. prepared mustard
1/4 c. mayonnaise
2 tsp. vinegar
1/2 tsp. seasoned salt

10 slices boiled ham
2 tbsp. finely chopped onion
1 tbsp. chopped pimentos
1/8 tsp. minced dillweed
1 can cream of mushroom soup
2/3 c. evaporated milk

Cut the eggs in half lengthwise and remove yolks. Mash the yolks in a bowl. Add 2 tablespoons parsley, mustard, mayonnaise, vinegar and seasoned salt and mix well. Fill egg whites with yolk mixture and place 2 halves together. Place each egg diagonally on 1 ham slice. Fold ham around egg and secure with toothpicks. Place in 12 x 7 1/2 x 2-inch baking dish. Combine remaining ingredients and remaining parsley and pour over eggs. Bake at 350 degrees for 20 to 25 minutes. 8-10 servings.

Mrs. Bill Stout, Piedmont, Oklahoma

HAM-ASPARAGUS CASSEROLE

1 can cream of mushroom soup
1/3 c. light cream
2 c. diced cooked ham

1 c. chopped cooked asparagus
Buttered bread crumbs

Blend the soup with cream. Add the ham and asparagus and mix well. Pour into a shallow baking dish and cover with crumbs. Bake at 375 degrees for 20 minutes. 4 servings.

Polly Johnson Hanst, Accident, Maryland

BAKED FISH IN CHEESE SAUCE

2 tbsp. butter or margarine	1 c. milk
3 tbsp. flour	3/4 tsp. lemon juice
3/4 tsp. salt	1/2 c. grated cheese
1/8 tsp. nutmeg	2 lb. fish fillets
1/2 tsp. dry mustard	

Melt the butter in a saucepan and blend in flour, salt, nutmeg and mustard. Stir in the milk and cook until thickened, stirring constantly. Add the lemon juice and cheese and stir until cheese is melted. Place the fish fillets in a greased casserole and cover with cheese sauce. Bake at 375 degrees for 45 minutes. 6 servings.

Mrs. Gerald A. Liechty, Belvidere, Tennessee

BAKED SHAD WITH DRESSING

1 4 to 5-lb. shad, dressed	1 tsp. parsley flakes
Salt and pepper to taste	1/2 c. diced celery
2 c. toasted bread crumbs	2 strips bacon
2 tbsp. melted butter or	5 med. onions
margarine	5 med. potatoes

Preheat oven to 325 degrees. Sprinkle the shad with salt and pepper and cut crosswise 3 times, 2 inches apart, through thick part of shad. Mix the bread crumbs with enough warm water to moisten. Add the butter, parsley, celery, salt and pepper and mix well. Place in cavity of shad and place bacon on top of shad. Place in a baking pan. Place the onions and potatoes around shad and add enough warm water to cover bottom of pan. Bake for 2 hours, basting occasionally and adding water, if needed. 6 servings.

Mrs. Carl Windbey, Pantego, North Carolina

SCALLOPED TUNA AND CHIPS

1/4 c. shortening	2 tbsp. grated onion
1/4 c. flour	1 tbsp. chopped parsley
1 tsp. salt	1 8-oz. package potato
1/8 tsp. pepper	chips, crushed
2 c. milk	2 7-oz. cans tuna

Melt the shortening in a saucepan. Add flour, salt and pepper and blend well. Add the milk and cook, stirring, until thickened. Remove from heat. Add onion and parsley and mix well. Place 1/3 of the potato chips in a greased 1 1/2-quart baking dish. Drain and flake the tuna and place half the tuna over potato chips. Add half the sauce. Repeat layers, ending with potato chips. Bake at 350 degrees for 1 hour. 6 servings.

Diane Suggett, Brinkley, Arkansas

SEAFOOD CREAM WITH AVOCADO HALVES

1 lb. fresh mushrooms,
  sliced
1 c. sliced onion
1 c. butter or margarine
2/3 c. flour
2 1/2 tsp. salt
1 tsp. monosodium glutamate
1/2 tsp. dry mustard
1/2 tsp. pepper
1/4 tsp. thyme leaves
5 c. milk
2 c. light cream

2 eggs, slightly beaten
2 c. grated Swiss cheese
8 7-oz. cans solid white
  tuna
1 c. sauterne
2 tsp. grated lemon peel
Lemon juice
6 5-oz. cans lobster, drained
2/3 c. chopped toasted
  blanched almonds
12 ripe avocados
Watercress

Saute the mushrooms and onion in butter until lightly browned and remove with slotted spoon. Quickly stir in the flour and seasonings. Stir in the milk and cream gradually. Cook and stir until the sauce boils for 1 minute. Stir a small amount of hot sauce into eggs and then return to the saucepan. Stir the cheese into hot sauce over low heat until melted. Drain the tuna and separate into large pieces. Add sauterne, lemon peel, 2 tablespoons lemon juice, tuna, lobster, almonds, sauteed mushrooms and onion to the sauce. Heat to serving temperature. Cut the avocados in half lengthwise, twisting gently to separate halves. Whack a sharp knife directly into seeds and twist to lift out. Peel avocado halves and brush with lemon juice. Arrange on a serving platter with watercress. Garnish with lime slices. Serve hot seafood mixture over avocado halves. Garnish with buttered, toasted fine bread crumbs and sliced truffles. 24 servings.

Photograph for this recipe on page 145.

CRAB MEAT AU GRATIN

Butter
2/3 c. flour
2 tsp. salt
2 2/3 c. milk
2 6 1/2-oz. cans crab meat
4 c. chopped celery
1/2 c. chopped green pepper

2 pimentos, drained and chopped
2 tbsp. grated onion
1/3 c. slivered toasted almonds
4 hard-cooked eggs, chopped
1 c. grated sharp Cheddar cheese
2 1/2 c. bread cubes

Melt 1/2 cup butter in a saucepan. Add the flour and salt and blend well. Add the milk gradually and cook, stirring constantly, until thick. Remove cartilage from crab meat and discard. Flake the crab meat and add to sauce. Stir in the celery, green pepper, pimentos, onion, almonds and eggs and place in a shallow 2-quart casserole. Sprinkle with cheese. Heat 1 tablespoon butter in a skillet. Add the bread cubes and toss until coated. Spoon onto cheese. Bake at 350 degrees for 35 minutes. 8-10 servings.

Mrs. Eugene Sloan, Paducah, Kentucky

CRAB BILOXI

1 6-oz. can crab meat
2 hard-cooked eggs, chopped
1 med. onion, chopped
1 med. green pepper, chopped
1 sprig of parsley, chopped
Juice of 1 lemon

1 tsp. Worcestershire sauce
2 eggs, beaten
1/2 c. mayonnaise
2 tbsp. melted butter
1 c. bread crumbs

Mix all ingredients except butter and bread crumbs and place in a greased casserole. Mix the butter and bread crumbs and sprinkle over casserole. Bake at 350 degrees for 30 minutes. 6 servings.

Cornelia S. Hegman, Holly Bluff, Mississippi

EASY RIPE OLIVE JAMBALAYA

1/4 c. chopped bacon
3 tbsp. chopped onion
3 tbsp. chopped green
   pepper
1 clove of garlic, minced
1 tbsp. flour
1/2 tsp. salt
Dash of cayenne pepper

Dash of paprika
1/2 tsp. Worcestershire
   sauce
1 1/2 c. canned pitted ripe
   olives
1 1-lb. can tomatoes
2 c. cooked rice
3/4 lb. cooked cleaned shrimp

Fry the bacon in a skillet until crisp. Add the onion, green pepper and garlic and cook until tender. Blend in the flour, salt, cayenne pepper, paprika and Worcestershire sauce. Cut the ripe olives in halves and add to bacon mixture. Stir in tomatoes and cook until thickened, stirring constantly. Add the rice and shrimp and mix. Place in a casserole. Bake at 350 degrees until heated through. 6 servings.

Photograph for this recipe on page 174.

LOBSTER-ARTICHOKE CASSEROLE

2 9-oz. packages frozen
   artichokes
Seasoned salt to taste
2 4 1/2-oz. packages precooked
   rice
3 5-oz. cans lobster

2 cans cream of mushroom soup
2 soup cans water
Triangles of American process
   cheese
Chopped parsley to taste

Cook the artichokes according to package directions and place in a 3-quart casserole. Sprinkle with seasoned salt and rice. Drain the lobster and place over rice. Blend the mushroom soup and water and pour over lobster. Bake at 400 degrees for 40 minutes. Top with cheese and sprinkle with parsley.

Mrs. Raymond Miles, Headland, Alabama

PAELLA

1 10 1/2-oz. can chicken
  broth
1/8 tsp. powdered saffron
8 chicken legs, cut apart
  at joint
Paprika to taste
1/4 c. olive oil
2 tsp. salt
1/2 lb. Spanish sausage,
  sliced
2 8-oz. packages frozen
  lobster-tails, thawed
1 clove of garlic, crushed

2 c. chopped green pepper
2 c. chopped onion
1 1/2 c. rice
1 c. dry white wine
1 16-oz. can tomatoes
1 1/2 c. small stuffed
  olives
1 tsp. chopped capers
1/2 tsp. pepper
1/2 tsp. oregano leaves
12 littleneck clams or
  mussels
1/2 c. frozen peas, thawed

Combine the chicken broth and saffron and let stand. Sprinkle the chicken with paprika and brown well on all sides in hot oil in large skillet. Sprinkle chicken with 1 teaspoon salt. Add the sausage and cover. Cook over low heat for 30 minutes or until chicken is tender. Remove sausage and chicken. Cut lobster-tails in half or thirds, if large, and place in same skillet. Saute until shells turn bright red and set aside with chicken. Drain off all except 1/2 cup drippings from skillet. Add the garlic, green pepper and onion to skillet and cook, stirring occasionally, until vegetables are crisp-tender. Add the rice and saute until opaque. Stir in the broth mixture, wine, tomatoes, olives, capers, pepper, oregano and remaining salt and cover. Cook over low heat for 15 minutes or until liquid is almost absorbed. Stir with a fork. Arrange the sausage, chicken and lobster over rice mixture and press into the mixture. Arrange clams over rice mixture so that shells touch edge of skillet and sprinkle the peas over rice mixture. Cover. Bake at 350 degrees for 15 minutes or until clams open and rice is tender.

Paella (above)

183

Oriental Chicken Casserole (below)

ORIENTAL CHICKEN CASSEROLE

1 c. sliced celery	2 tsp. soy sauce
1/2 c. green onion slices,	1/2 c. shredded American
1/2 in. long	process cheese
1/3 c. butter	2 c. diced cooked chicken
1/4 c. flour	1 8-oz. can water
1 tsp. salt	chestnuts
Dash of garlic salt	1 6-oz. can chow mein
2 c. milk	noodles

Saute the celery and onion slices in butter in a saucepan until onion is soft.
Blend in the flour, salt and garlic salt. Add milk and soy sauce and cook, stirring
constantly, until thickened. Remove from heat. Add the cheese and stir until
melted. Stir in the chicken and water chestnuts. Arrange alternate layers of
noodles and chicken mixture in a 1 1/2-quart casserole, beginning and ending
with noodles. Bake at 375 degrees for 25 to 30 minutes or until hot and bubbly.
6 servings.

COUNTRY CLUB CHICKEN SCALLOP

1 c. butter or margarine	10 c. chicken broth
1 tsp. celery salt	7 c. milk
1 tsp. rubbed sage	12 c. chopped cooked chicken
1 tsp. poultry seasoning	5 c. toasted bread crumbs
2 c. flour	2 cans onion rings

Melt the butter in a large saucepan and stir in the celery salt, sage, poultry
seasoning and flour. Add the broth and milk and cook, stirring constantly, until

thickened. Place alternate layers of chicken, crumbs and sauce in greased baking pans. Top with onion rings. Bake at 350 degrees for 30 minutes. 30 servings.

Mrs. M. I. Stutler, Clarksburg, West Virginia

CHICKEN-TACO CASSEROLE

1 3-lb. chicken, cooked	Dash of pepper
2 cans enchilada sauce	1 sm. package corn chips
1 can mushroom soup	1 c. grated cheese
1 lge. onion, chopped	1 c. chicken broth
1/2 tsp. garlic salt	

Remove chicken from bones and cut in bite-sized pieces. Combine the chicken, enchilada sauce, soup, onion, garlic salt and pepper. Place half the corn chips in a greased baking dish. Add chicken mixture and sprinkle with cheese. Cover with remaining corn chips and pour broth over top. Bake at 350 degrees for about 30 minutes. 6-8 servings.

Mrs. Ersel Tice, Logan, Oklahoma

CHICKEN VA-TEL

4 chicken breasts	1 c. milk
2 c. water	Salt to taste
2 tbsp. butter	1/4 c. grated cheese
1 sm. package egg noodles	

Cook the chicken in water and butter in a saucepan until tender. Drain and reserve broth. Remove chicken from bones and cut in small pieces. Cook the noodles according to package directions and drain. Place alternate layers of chicken and noodles in a baking dish. Add milk, reserved chicken broth and salt and sprinkle cheese on top. Bake at 350 degrees for 25 minutes. 6 servings.

Mrs. T. J. Land, Canton, Georgia

GREEN PEPPERS-CHICKEN AU GRATIN

6 green peppers	6 hard-cooked eggs, sliced
1 onion, chopped fine	1/4 lb. cheese, grated
3 tbsp. butter or shortening	2 c. strained tomatoes
1 c. chopped cooked chicken	Salt and pepper to taste
1 1/2 c. whole wheat bread crumbs	1 tsp. Worcestershire sauce

Slice the green peppers crosswise. Cook in small amount of water in a saucepan for 5 minutes and drain. Saute the green peppers and onion in butter until tender, then place in a baking dish. Cover with chicken and 1 cup crumbs. Place eggs over chicken mixture and add the cheese. Combine the tomatoes, salt, pepper and Worcestershire sauce and pour over cheese. Sprinkle with remaining crumbs and dot with additional butter. Bake at 375 degrees for 30 minutes.

Robina C. Whitley, Majestic, Kentucky

HOT TURKEY SALAD SOUFFLE

6 thin slices bread	3/4 tsp. salt
2 c. diced cooked turkey	Dash of pepper
1/2 c. chopped onion	2 eggs, beaten
1/2 c. chopped green pepper	1 1/2 c. milk
1/2 c. chopped celery	1 c. cream of mushroom soup
1/2 c. mayonnaise	1/2 c. shredded cheese

Cut 2 slices bread in cubes and place in an 8 x 8 x 2-inch baking dish. Combine the turkey, vegetables, mayonnaise and seasonings and spoon over bread cubes. Trim crusts from remaining bread and arrange on turkey mixture. Combine the eggs and milk and pour over bread. Cover with foil and chill overnight. Spoon soup over top. Bake at 325 degrees for 1 hour or until set. Sprinkle cheese over top and bake for 15 minutes longer or until brown. 6 servings.

Mrs. Walter C. Robert, Talequah, Oklahoma

BAKED MACARONI AND TOMATOES AU GRATIN

4 tbsp. butter or margarine	2 15-oz. cans macaroni with
2 tbsp. dry bread crumbs	cheese sauce
1/4 c. chopped onion	3 hard-cooked eggs, sliced
1/4 c. sour cream	1 lge. tomato, sliced
1/2 tsp. salt	Parsley sprigs
Dash of cayenne pepper	

Preheat oven to 350 degrees. Melt the butter in a small skillet. Remove 2 table-spoons, toss with bread crumbs and reserve. Saute onion in remaining butter for about 3 minutes or until golden. Remove from heat. Add the sour cream, salt and cayenne pepper and mix well. Place 1 can macaroni in a 1 1/2-quart casserole and add 2 eggs. Add sour cream mixture. Add remaining macaroni and arrange tomato slices around edge. Sprinkle with reserved crumbs. Bake for 30 to 35 minutes or until hot and bubbly. Garnish with remaining egg and parsley. 6 servings.

Mrs. G. L. Shoemake, Yazoo City, Mississippi

BAKED ONIONS WITH MUSTARD SAUCE

6 lge. mild onions	2 tbsp. chopped parsley
1 c. toasted bread cubes	1/4 tsp. poultry seasoning
1/4 c. melted butter	1/4 tsp. salt
Dash of pepper	Mustard Sauce

Cook the onions in boiling, salted water for about 30 minutes or until tender. Drain and cool. Remove centers. Mix the bread cubes, butter, pepper, parsley, poultry seasoning and salt and place in cavities of onions. Place close together in a greased casserole. Bake at 350 degrees for about 30 minutes. Serve with Mustard Sauce.

Baked Onions with Mustard Sauce (page 186)

Mustard Sauce

2 1/2 tbsp. butter

2 1/2 tbsp. flour

1/2 tsp. salt

Dash of pepper

1 1/2 c. milk

1 tbsp. prepared mustard

2 tbsp. lemon juice

Melt the butter in a saucepan over low heat and blend in the flour, salt and pepper. Add the milk slowly and cook, stirring constantly, until smooth and thickened. Blend in the mustard. Add lemon juice, slowly, stirring constantly.

BUFFET CHEESE AND CARROTS

12 med. carrots

1 sm. onion, minced

1/4 c. butter or margarine

1/4 c. flour

1 tsp. salt

1/4 tsp. dry mustard

2 c. milk

1/8 tsp. pepper

1/4 tsp. celery salt

1/2 lb. American process
    cheese slices

3 c. buttered bread crumbs

Slice the carrots. Cook in boiling water for 15 minutes and drain. Cook the onion in butter in a saucepan for 2 to 3 minutes. Stir in the flour, salt and mustard. Add the milk and cook, stirring, until smooth and thickened. Add pepper and celery salt. Place 1/3 of the carrots in a 2-quart casserole and add half the cheese. Repeat layers, ending with carrots. Pour sauce over carrots and top with crumbs. Bake at 350 degrees for about 25 minutes or until crumbs are golden brown. 6-8 servings.

Mrs. George L. Shank, Williamsport, Maryland

DILLED GREEN BEANS

2 cans sliced green beans	3 tbsp. grated onion
1 tsp. dillseed	2 tsp. monosodium glutamate
1 tbsp. bacon drippings	Salt and pepper to taste
6 tbsp. margarine	Dash of hot sauce
6 tbsp. flour	Buttered bread crumbs
1 c. milk	

Place the beans, dillseed and bacon drippings in a saucepan and cook until liquid is reduced to 1 cup. Drain and reserve liquid. Place the beans in a casserole. Melt the margarine in a saucepan and blend in flour. Stir in reserved bean liquid, milk, onion, monosodium glutamate, salt, pepper and hot sauce and cook until thick, stirring constantly. Pour over beans. Cover casserole with crumbs. Bake at 350 degrees for 20 to 25 minutes. 6-8 servings.

Mrs. Ernest Highers, Ozark, Arkansas

MUSHROOM-CHEESE CASSEROLE

1 c. grated Swiss cheese	1 tbsp. chopped green onion (opt.)
1 1/2 c. soft bread cubes	3 eggs, separated
1 3-oz. can broiled mushrooms	1/2 tsp. salt
1/2 c. milk	1/2 tsp. prepared mustard
2 tbsp. butter or margarine	

Reserve 2 tablespoons cheese. Combine remaining cheese, bread cubes, mushrooms and liquid, milk and butter in a saucepan and cook over low heat, stirring occasionally until cheese and butter are melted. Cool and add onion. Beat the egg yolks with salt and mustard in a large bowl, then add cheese mixture gradually. Beat egg whites until stiff but not dry and fold into cheese mixture. Pour into a shallow 1-quart casserole and top with reserved cheese. Bake at 350 degrees for 30 to 35 minutes. Serve immediately. 4 servings.

Photograph for this recipe on page 86.

POLYNESIAN RICE

1 c. wild rice	1/4 c. soy sauce
1 c. rice	1/2 c. chopped macadamia or
1/4 c. minced onion	cashew nuts
1 can beef consomme	1/4 c. chopped parsley
2 3/4 c. water	

Preheat oven to 350 degrees. Combine the wild rice, rice and onion in a 2-quart casserole. Mix the consomme, water and soy sauce and pour over rice mixture. Cover. Bake for 1 hour, then sprinkle with nuts and parsley. 8 servings.

Clariece Quintana, Santa Fe, New Mexico

INDEX

Apple Desserts
poached in orange juice, 98
slices, skillet, 98
Banana Flambe, Rio, 96
BEEF
barbecued beef buns, 121
casseroles
Parmigiana, 176
peach pie, 176
shepherd's pie, 177
souffle, 177
Spanish, 177
continental, 121
curry, Bongsor, 121
fondues
Burgundy, 12
corned beef balls, delicious, 18
international, 13
mustard-curry, 14
sirloin supreme, 16
steak, marinated, 13
with hot gazpacho sauce, 14
with sauces, 12
ground beef, see "Ground Beef"
short ribs
with raisin sauce, 122
with vegetables, 123
soy, with green peas, 122
steak
Algerienne, 123
creole, 124
Madeira, 124
pepper, Chinese, 136
round, stuffed, 123
sukiyaki, 137
with dumplings, 122
yakitizers, 136
BEVERAGES
apple cider
fondue beverage, 40
range, 42
cafe, 40
cherry punch, mulled, 41
chocolate, hot, at-the-table, 40
Jamaican blazer, 40
tea, Russian, 42
wassail bowl, 41
BREADS
biscuits
cheese, 160
herbed pinwheels, 160
breadsticks, herb, 163
buns, fruit, Bohemian, 162
muffins
bran, delicious, 161
carrot, 161
cranberry-pumpkin, 161
nut horns, Danish, 162
Swedish, 163
Brownies, blonde, 168
CAKES
blueberry holiday ring, 165
bourbon-raisin, 164

holiday, 164
petits fours, 166
pound, brown sugar, 164
CHEESE FONDUES
au vin, 24
double, 29
Geneva, 26
hot dip, 28
Italian, 27
mushroom-Cheddar, 25
Neuchatel-style, 27
nippy, 28
pizza, 28
quick, 24
rarebit
crab, for buffet, 25
Welsh, 55
first-rate, 28
savant, Pat's, 24
spiced, classic, 24
Swiss, family-style, 26
tomato, 29
tuna, 25
Cherry Desserts
almond jubilee, 98
cerise noir, 96
CHICKEN
and dumplings, 117
arroz caldo, 115
captain's, 112
casseroles
green peppers au gratin, 185
oriental, 184
scallop, country club, 184
taco, 185
va-tel, 185
Charlotte Louise, 112
creamed, over croutons, 114
deviled, 114
fondues
en barde, 18
jet-set, 17
in raisin sauce, supreme, 113
livers
in sour cream, 116
party, 116
New Delhi, 114
with noodles
Cheddar, chafing dish, 115
tetrazzini, chafing dish, 115
with Taiwan rice, 140
Coffee-Chocolate Cream, 169
Cranberry Flambe, crimson, 100
Crepes
apple, fresh, 96
lime, 98
Suzette, 102
Custards
butterscotch cream, 102
creme brulee, 168
DESSERT FONDUES
banana scallop, 47
cheese, three, 46

chocolate
    marshmallow, 48
    marveilleuse, 49
    peach, 48
fruit pies, fried, 45
fruity fritters, 46
minted, 47
orange, tangy, 48
peaches Chantilly with sauce, 44
strawberry, 47
DIPS
    bean
        and bacon, 54
        caliente sauce, 54
    cheese
        clam-garlic, 56
        cocheese chili, 55
        diablo, 54
        Mexican, 56
        onion fromage, 56
        smokey bacon, 54
    shrimp, gulf, 60
EGGS
    deviled, holiday, hot, 93
    joyale, 90
    le grande, 90
    omelet
        French, 90
        with cheese sauce, baked, 91
    scrambled
        almond, delicious, 92
        and salmon, peppered, 93
        Gruyere, 92
        herbed, 92
        Louisianne, 92
        Point Clear, 90
    shirred, Montmorency, 93
Figs in Cream, chafing dish, 96
FISH
    casseroles
        baked, in cheese sauce, 180
        seafood cream with avocado
            halves, 181
        shad, baked with dressing, 180
        tuna and chips, scalloped, 180
    flounder, fillet, 108
    fondues
        salmon, 19
            fish and shrimp, 20
            jubilee, 109
            scallop, crunchy, 108
        spiced, 108
Fruit-Champagne Compote, mixed, 166
Grits
    au gratin, 70
    cheese, 70
    tomato, and cheese, 70
GROUND BEEF
    Greco, 124
    meatballs
        Belgian, 124
        ripe olive, international, 120
    stroganoff, 126
    tacos, ripe olive, 125
HAM
    balls and Louisiana yams, 129
    casseroles

and baked deviled eggs, 179
    apple, 179
    asparagus, 179
country ham with raisin sauce, 128
rolls, stuffed, chafing dish, 130
with miniature tart shells, 129
HORS D'OEUVRES
    almonds, cocktail, 56
    chicken
        and oysters a la king, 58
        in canape shells, 59
        livers
            broiled, 57
            chestnuts, savory, 59
    meat
        bacon roll-ups, 57
        frankfurters, tiny battered, 15
        meatballs, sweet and sour, 58
        Polynesian, 57
        sausages Italiano, 58
    seafood
        poisson a coquilles in wine, 60
        rock lobster, 60
        salmon blintzes, 61
LAMB
    and rice, fried, 131
    and vegetables orientale,
        gingered, 138
    curry, 131
        raisin, with Persian rice, 130
    fondue, 17
    kabobs, 139
    patties with currant sauce, 131
Macaroni
    and tomatoes au gratin, baked, 186
    Milano, 73
    pasta jambalaya, 72
Meringues
    strawberry cream in Swiss
        meringues, 169
Moose Fondue, 16
NOODLES
    Alfredo, 74
    fettucine in tuna sauce, 74
    pancakes, party, 73
    Parmesan, buttered, 74
    Valienti, 74
PEACH DESSERTS
    brandy, 101
    fresh peach-raspberry mold, 166
    mincemeat flambe, 100
    orange crumble, 101
Pear Desserts
    chocolate, 100
    Milanese, stuffed, 100
Pies
    caramel pecan, 171
    chocolate chip-almond, 171
    lemon, perfect, 171
Pineapple-Banana Charlotte, 167
PORK
    casseroles
        rice, Paula, 178
        sweet potato buffet, 178
    chops
        and broccoli, 126
        lemon-smothered, 127

Spanish, 127
    sweet potato dinner, 127
chop suey, 138
cubes with pineapple, 128
gai lo mein, 138
ham, see "Ham"
sausage with spaghetti, chafing
    dish, 130
steaks, braised, 126
sweet and sour supreme, 128
won ton fry, 138

Puddings
cottage, with blueberry sauce, 102

RICE
almond, 71
exotic casserole, 72
green, 71
Polynesian, 188
rajahmundry, 70
Spanish, pronto, 71
wild, epicurean, 72
with ham, party, 71

SALADS
chicken
    almond-sesame, 152
    curried, grape mingle, 151
    en cornucopia, 152
    Sorrento, 151
fruit
    Antigua, 150
    avocado ring with frosted
        fruits, 148
    congealed, with fresh fruit, 149
    golden Floridian, 150
    orange-fig ring, 150
    peach in wine jelly, buffet, 148
    strawberry glace, 149
    with cheese, 150
meat
    beef, jellied, 153
    pork crown, party, 153
    veal, jellied, 152
seafood
    crab
        aspic, 154
        double summer salad, 154
        Louis, 153
    lobster, 154
    remoulade, 156
    salmon with cucumber dressing,
        cold, 155
    tuna-potato, German, 155
vegetable
    bean, creole, 156
    potato ensalada, 156
    spinach mold, sea breeze, 157
    tomato sambal, 157

SAUCES
applesauce, spiced winter, 45
butterscotch dessert fondue, 44
caramel nut, 42
cranberry, gourmet, 42
honey
    Indienne spiced, 43
    orange, 45
orange-maple sucre, 43
sundae, Hawaiian, 43

SHELLFISH
casseroles
    crab
        au gratin, 181
        Biloxi, 182
    lobster-artichoke, 182
    paella, 183
    ripe olive jambalaya, easy, 182
coquille St. Jacques, 109
crab
    balls in sauce, 106
    imperial, 106
    Jacques, 106
curried seafood, 111
fondues
    lobster, 20
    shrimp
        crevettes, toasted, 20
        fish, 20
        Romano, 18
lobster
    buffet, 107
    kabobs, hibachi, 141
    Newberg, 109
oysters
    Blandine, 110
    jambalaya, 110
shrimp
    balls, 110
    Chinese, 140
    creole delight, 110
    skewered, 141
    stroganoff, 112
    tempura, Shino, 140

SOUPS
beef
    Flemish, 79
    green beans Fagidini, 81
    Mexican, de albondigas, 80
    tomato mouseron, 81
chicken
    avgolemono, 78
    Mediterranean sandwich soup, 78
chili, chafing dish, 80
chowders
    clam, 87
    corn
        and dried beef, 87
        fresh
            seafood, 86
    Roan, 87
clam-tomato, 82
goulash with noodles, 80
gumbo
    chicken and oyster, 79
    creole, 82
oxtail, 81
salmon, 83
shrimp bisque, springtime, 83
vegetable
    asparagus, creamy, 83
    bean
        chafing dish, 83
        pasta fagioli, 84
    borsch with sour cream, 85
    corn
        cheese, 84

maize, 84
onion-chicken, au vin, 85
pea
    supreme, 85
    with mushrooms, 85
Spaghetti
oyster Luisa, 75
with chicken livers, 75
with frankfurters, 75
Strawberry Omelet, flaming, 103
TARTS
blueberry-cream cheese pastries, 173
date, 172
lemon chess, 172
strawberry mocha cream tartlets, 172
Tortes
raisin-coconut, 170
sour cream, 170
Tortoni, Bisque, 168
Turkey
feuillete, 117
salad souffle, hot, 186
VEAL
casseroles
    and rice, 178
    chops, 178
Parmesan, 126
VEGETABLES
asparagus, gourmet, 64
beans, Turkish, 65
beets
    marinated, 65
    with pineapple, golden glory, 69
casseroles
    carrots and cheese, buffet, 187
    green beans, dilled, 188

mushroom-cheese, 188
onions baked with mustard
    sauce, 186
cauliflower
spiced, 66
with Peter Pancho sauce, 66
eggplant Capri, 65
fondues
artichokes with Swiss fondue, 34
beans
    green, flavor-full, 36
    with rinktum ditty, 37
carrots and artichoke hearts, 34
cauliflower
    cheese, 33
    salad fritters, 33
celery in shrimp fondue, 33
curry, 32
eggplant, crisp, 35
mushroom, 34
onion-bacon, 35
potatoes
    marines, 36
    tiny, in curry sauce, 36
tomato-Parmesan, 36
mushrooms and eggs in cheese sauce
    supreme, 64
potatoes
au gratin, 68
creamed hash, 68
pancakes
    onion, 67
ratatouille, 67
succotash, 67
sweet potatoes
Alexandria, 68
naranja, 68

PHOTOGRAPHY CREDITS: Bluebonnet Margarine; Planter's Peanut Oil; Fleischmann's Margarine; National Association of Frozen Food Packers; International Tuna Fish Association; National Cherries Growers and Industries Foundation; National Macaroni Institute; California Strawberry Advisory Board; Best Foods: A Division of Corn Products Company International; South African Rock Lobster Service Corporation; American Dairy Association; U. S. Department of Commerce: National Marine Fisheries Service; The Apple Pantry: Washington State Apple Commission; Sterno Canned Heat; Florida Citrus Commission; Knox Gelatine; United Fresh Fruit and Vegetable Association; Ocean Spray Cranberries, Inc.; The R. T. French Company; North American Blueberry Council; National Dairy Council; Campbell Soup Company; Artichoke Advisory Board; Peter Pan Peanut Butter; Spanish Green Olive Commission; Louisiana Yam Commission; Idaho Bean Commission; Western Growers Association; Cling Peach Advisory Board; McIlhenny Company; Grandma's West Indies Molasses; Pineapple Growers Association; Olive Administrative Committee; Fleischmann's Yeast; Canned Salmon Institute; California Prune Advisory Board; California Raisin Advisory Board; American Lamb Council; American Dry Milk Institute.

Printed in the United States of America.